Kirsten Dunst

Kirsten Dunst

Titles in the People in the News series include:

PEOPLE
IN THE NEWS

Kirsten Dunst

by Anne E. Hill

3SLAD00065694J

92
DUNST

LUCENT BOOKS

An imprint of Thomson Gale, a part of The Thomson Corporation

THOMSON
™
GALE

Detroit • New York • San Francisco • San Diego • New Haven, Conn.
Waterville, Maine • London • Munich

To my wonderful Caleb and your future little sister.

© 2005 Thomson Gale, a part of The Thomson Corporation.

Thomson and Star Logo are trademarks and Gale and Lucent Books are registered trademarks used herein under license.

For more information, contact
Lucent Books
27500 Drake Rd.
Farmington Hills, MI 48331-3535
Or you can visit our Internet site at http://www.gale.com

LIBRARY OF CONGRESS CATALOGING-IN-PUBLICATION DATA

Hill, Anne E., 1974–
  Kirsten Dunst / by Anne E. Hill.
    p. cm. — (People in the news)
  Includes bibliographical references and index.
  ISBN 1-59018-715-6 (hard cover : alk. paper)
1. Dunst, Kirsten, 1982—Juvenile literature. 2. Motion picture actors and actresses—United States—Biography—Juvenile literature. I. Title. II. Series: People in the news (San Diego, CA.)
PN2287.D854H55 2005
791.4302'8'092—dc22

                                                                    2004026873

Printed in the United States of America

Table of Contents

Foreword

FAME AND CELEBRITY are alluring. People are drawn to those who walk in fame's spotlight, whether they are known for great accomplishments or for notorious deeds. The lives of the famous pique public interest and attract attention, perhaps because their experiences seem in some ways so different from, yet in other ways so similar to, our own.

Newspapers, magazines, and television regularly capitalize on this fascination with celebrity by running profiles of famous people. For example, television programs such as *Entertainment Tonight* devote all of their programming to stories about entertainment and entertainers. Magazines such as *People* fill their pages with stories of the private lives of famous people. Even newspapers, newsmagazines, and television news frequently delve into the lives of well-known personalities. Despite the number of articles and programs, few provide more than a superficial glimpse at their subjects.

Lucent's People in the News series offers young readers a deeper look into the lives of today's newsmakers, the influences that have shaped them, and the impact they have had in their fields of endeavor and on other people's lives. The subjects of the series hail from many disciplines and walks of life. They include authors, musicians, athletes, political leaders, entertainers, entrepreneurs, and others who have made a mark on modern life and who, in many cases, will continue to do so for years to come.

These biographies are more than factual chronicles. Each book emphasizes the contributions, accomplishments, or deeds that have brought fame or notoriety to the individual and shows how that person has influenced modern life. Authors portray their subjects in a realistic, unsentimental light. For example, Bill Gates—the cofounder and chief executive officer of the software giant Microsoft—has been instrumental in making personal computers the most vital tool of the modern age. Few dispute his business savvy, his perseverance, or his technical expertise, yet critics say he is ruthless in his dealings with competitors and driven more by his desire to maintain Microsoft's dominance in the computer industry than by an interest in furthering technology.

In these books, young readers will encounter inspiring stories about real people who achieved success despite enormous obstacles. Oprah Winfrey–the most powerful, most watched, and wealthiest woman on television today–spent the first six years of her life in the care of her grandparents while her unwed mother sought work and a better life elsewhere. Her adolescence was colored by promiscuity, pregnancy at age fourteen, rape, and sexual abuse.

Each author documents and supports his or her work with an array of primary and secondary source quotations taken from diaries, letters, speeches, and interviews. All quotes are footnoted to show readers exactly how and where biographers derive their information and provide guidance for further research. The quotations enliven the text by giving readers eyewitness views of the life and accomplishments of each person covered in the People in the News series.

In addition, each book in the series includes photographs, annotated bibliographies, timelines, and comprehensive indexes. For both the casual reader and the student researcher, the People in the News series offers insight into the lives of today's newsmakers–people who shape the way we live, work, and play in the modern age.

Introduction

"Spanning the Decades"

STILL IN HER early twenties, Kirsten Dunst has done the near impossible in Hollywood—she has gone from a perky toddler in TV commercials to the A-list star of top-grossing films. In a career that spans two decades, Dunst has made such blockbusters as the *Spider-Man* films, small independent films such as *The Virgin Suicides* and *The Cat's Meow*, as well as films that appeal to young viewers, such as the cheerleader flick *Bring It On*. Her versatility has kept her in demand and working nonstop. It has also expanded her fan base to include both kids and adults. But it has not always been easy working in the competitive field of acting, and Dunst has made some sacrifices along the way.

Dunst started making commercials when most kids her age were in preschool. As a child, Dunst appeared in more than seventy television ads, graduating to feature films well before high school. When Dunst was very young, her ambitions led to teasing by her classmates and she experienced rejection at many auditions, but the little actress had found her calling and never considered doing anything else.

Highly photogenic and a gifted actress, Dunst became popular with moviegoers when *Interview with the Vampire* was released in 1994. For her performance in the costume horror film based on Anne Rice's best-selling novel of the same name, Dunst was nominated for a Golden Globe Award, and won the MTV Movie Award for Best Breakthrough Performance and the Saturn Award for Best Actress. Nationally famous because

For an actress in her twenties, Kirsten Dunst has an impressive résumé. From childhood appearances in TV commercials, she went on to star in blockbuster movies.

of the role—which she embarked on at the age of ten—Dunst appeared in hits such as *Little Women*, *Jumanji*, *crazy/beautiful*, *Bring It On*, *Mona Lisa Smile*, and *Spider-Man*. More than forty films later, Dunst is one of the most sought-after young actresses in Hollywood, and at twenty-two, her career is only just beginning.

A millionaire many times over by the time she turned twenty, Dunst now commands $5 million per movie. She wears the newest and trendiest fashions from top designers, many of whom give their clothes to her at no charge. And with her enviable good looks, she often walks the red carpet with Hollywood's hottest young actors.

Indeed, Dunst's life may seem to be perfect. Even her longish eyeteeth, which she jokingly calls fangs, may have helped her land her important role as a vampire. Some have wondered if she will get them "fixed," but the answer is no; she likes her fangs. On the personal front, however, her parents' divorce in 1996 spawned painful rumors linking the breakup to her career success. Romantically, she has lived out an on-again, off-again relationship with actor Jake Gyllenhaal under an unwelcome amount of media attention. Careerwise, her lauded film debut may have been too much, too soon. Her early success set a very high standard in terms of quality projects she would perform in. And after some movies that went straight to video, she was typecast as a cute, bubbly blonde. Her role as a deep, brooding, and complex teen in Sofia Coppola's *The Virgin Suicides* put an end to that stereotype. Dunst's second big break, however, led to working at a breakneck pace on one movie after another that left her feeling mostly unfulfilled.

Dunst overcame this less-than-satisfying phase in her career by deciding to slow down, accepting only projects of the highest quality. Her decision paid off, and she has since become a true leading lady. Her career hit official superstar status when she was cast as Mary Jane Watson opposite Tobey Maguire's Spider-Man in the blockbuster film and its highly successful sequel. She also hit her stride as an actress, learning to communicate more effectively to directors and express her own ideas about storylines and her characters. She has acknowledged that she would love to direct, and perhaps someday she will put her mind to it. Dunst has already started her own production company called Wooden Spoon Productions to help herself and other female acting professionals select and develop the best roles for women.

Barely out of her teens, Kirsten Dunst is now in a position to pick and choose her own roles, in films as diverse as *Wimbledon, Elizabethtown,* and *Marie Antoinette.* And her fans are eager to see what she decides to do next. Having spent almost all of her life in the spotlight, Dunst cannot imagine living any other way.

Chapter 1

Already Acting

Unlike many actors and actresses who begin working at a very young age, Kirsten Dunst was not born into a show business family–and she was not born in the entertainment capitals of Los Angeles or New York City. But the path Kirsten would follow was clear from a very young age. Among the first to spot her flair for the dramatic was her mother, Inez Dunst, who told an interviewer, "Kirsten was born and seemed to know what she was going to do."[1]

Kirsten Caroline Dunst was born on April 30, 1982, in the small seaside resort town of Point Pleasant, New Jersey. The town's motto is "A nice place to visit, a great place to live." At just over a mile square and with only about five thousand year-round residents (the town's numbers grow significantly in the summer months, when seasonal residents and renters flood the town), Point Pleasant was a cozy place to live as well, a place where all the long-term residents know one another.

With her big blue-green eyes, dimples, and blonde ringlets, baby Kirsten was definitely noticed by her neighbors. She remembers, "People used to come up to my mother and say, 'Oh, does your daughter model?'"[2] Dunst's parents, Klaus, a medical services executive, and Inez, a homemaker who had once owned an art gallery, soon realized that their daughter might have a future in show business.

An Early Start

By the time Kirsten was three, it was obvious that she wanted to act: A natural mimic, she could imitate the expressions she saw and voices she heard with amazing accuracy. Inez took her to the prestigious Elite Modeling Agency in New York City, nearly fifty miles north of Point Pleasant. The staff there were so impressed by the little girl that they sent her out on auditions immediately.

Kirsten got her start in print ads and then moved on to the competitive world of television commercials. At each audition, Kirsten competed against dozens and dozens of cute children who could deliver their lines on cue, and she had more than a few disappointments. But she also had something special that got her noticed, and she eventually starred in more than seventy television ads. In the 1980s little Kirsten was all over television, helping sell everything from cold medicine to candy and toys. Two of the ads she remembers best were for a baby doll that peed and pooped in its diaper and for a pregnant doll that would "deliver" the baby when her tummy was pressed. Kirsten later realized that both products were more than a little strange.

Kirsten is pictured here at the age of twelve. At that point in her career, the actress had already appeared in dozens of commercials and played several roles in different movies.

But despite any reservations she may have had about the products she was helping to sell, Kirsten loved acting. Still very young, she wanted each job to last forever and hated when shooting ended on a commercial, especially if she did not have another job lined up for the near future. So when she was not acting in commercials, she directed her little cousins in living room plays. "I just enjoyed it so much," she says. "No one ever had to push me into anything. I loved going on auditions. It was so exciting to me. When I wasn't working, I'd be so upset. I cried when I couldn't go into New York and work."[3]

Trips to New York were a little harder to manage after Kirsten's little brother, Christian, was born in 1986, the year Kirsten started going to school. But Inez made the almost-daily commute into the city with her daughter and infant son. It was hard juggling the demands of Kirsten's career and a baby, but Inez was determined that her daughter should get to follow her

Inez Dunst (center) faced the challenge of raising Kirsten and her brother Christian (right) while advancing her daughter's career.

dreams, and Kirsten was thrilled with the experiences she was having. She enjoyed not only the work she was doing, but the fun time she got to spend with her family. "From where we lived in New Jersey, it was an hour and a half drive [into New York City]," Kirsten says. "My mom would pick me up after school. Sometimes my grandma would come, and we'd all sing in the car. We'd play 'Name That Tune' and sing *Les Miserables* or Madonna songs. I'd do my homework riding home at night."[4] Because Kirsten loved it so much and she was having so much success, Inez saw the family's sacrifices as worthwhile. Klaus, however, never thought his daughter's acting "hobby" would develop into a real career.

Other Genres

With dozens of TV commercials to her credit, Kirsten made the leap to the big screen with bit roles in films shot in and around New York City. She had a small role as Mia Farrow's character's daughter in the segment of the 1989 film *New York Stories* directed by Woody Allen. Next she played Tom Hanks's character's young daughter, Campbell McCoy, in *The Bonfire of the Vanities*. Although the film, directed by Brian DePalma and based on the best-selling novel by Tom Wolfe, was not well received by critics when it was released in 1990, it gave Kirsten valuable exposure in film.

New York City did not have quite as many television and film acting opportunities as Los Angeles, but Kirsten made the most of what was available. She guest starred on the soap opera *Loving* and had a bit appearance portraying one of George H.W. Bush's granddaughters on the sketch comedy show *Saturday Night Live*. She even got to utter the show's famous opening line: "Live from New York, it's Saturday night!" (Years later Kirsten would host the show herself, fulfilling a goal she had had since childhood.)

Kirsten also took on the role that gave her a nickname she still has to this day. After she did a voiceover for the title role in the American version of a Japanese animated film called *Kiki's Delivery Service*, her family and friends started calling her Kiki.

Now eight years old and a recognized actress, Kirsten was nevertheless a normal little girl who liked to turn popped balloons into rubber outfits for her Barbie dolls. Her professional career earned her some teasing by some of the other children at school, but Kirsten did find time to play with a few neighborhood friends. In any event, she was not about to give up acting just because she was called names on the playground. She was determined to live her dream. By 1990, however, that dream seemed to be stalled, since opportunities in New York for an actress Kirsten's age were limited.

The Big Move

Instead of giving up or continuing to struggle in New York, Inez decided to move to Los Angeles to give Kirsten's career a boost. More movies were made in L.A., and Kirsten had clearly taken her New York commercial and film career as far as it could go. Kirsten was still in elementary school when Inez moved to California with her children. Klaus Dunst stayed behind in New Jersey to keep his job and take care of the family's home, which they were not ready to sell. Inez and Klaus were having marital problems, and they thought that perhaps the move would also help them work out the problems in their relationship. It was more than a little scary for Inez to move across the country with two young children, but she was confident that Kirsten would have as much success on the West Coast as she had on the East.

The Dunsts' first year in California was difficult. Kirsten was still getting work, but it was primarily TV commercials and small roles in forgettable movies. The family was living at the Oakwood, an apartment complex filled with newly arrived young actors and actresses trying to make it in Hollywood. Little girls and boys were as competitive with each other after the auditions as they were on them. Pushy stage mothers did whatever they could to promote their children's career. Kirsten recalls: "I didn't love staying there. I didn't care for the atmosphere. You'd jump in the pool and kids would be, like, 'Oh, what movie are you in? What audition are you going on?' And all the mothers would be talking about 'What agency are you with?' It was so annoying."[5]

Kirsten even remembers one little girl, who did not realize who she was talking to, announcing that she was going to be the

Kirsten and Inez are pictured at an award show in Los Angeles, where the Dunst family moved in 1990 in search of new acting opportunities for Kirsten.

next Kirsten Dunst. Kirsten was surprised that the girl knew her name, as she hadn't had a main role in a feature film yet.

Some may have wondered if Inez was a pushy mom like some of the others at the Oakwood, but Kirsten insists that she herself wanted nothing more than to act and her mother had sacrificed everything, not the other way around. "If I'd wanted to go home one day, she'd have turned around and gone home,"

Shown at the premiere of Little Women *in 1994, Kirsten's big break came when she landed a big role in the hit movie* Interview with the Vampire.

she says. "There were times when I was discouraged with just auditioning, but then I got *Interview with the Vampire*."[6]

But before she got the role that would make her famous, Kirsten needed a new agent. Elite was known for its models, but Kirsten needed a Los Angeles–based agent who could help her find bigger roles in major films. Shortly after moving to Los Angeles, Kirsten and her mom met with the famous children's agent Iris Burton, who had discovered River Phoenix years earlier. Kirsten remembers the first meeting at a fast-food restaurant on Sunset Boulevard: "I was nine. She [Burton] made me get up, turn around and walk back. She was so excited for me to meet River."[7] Burton signed Kirsten, and shortly afterward, both Dunst and Phoenix were cast in *Interview with the Vampire*. Phoenix, however, died of a drug overdose in October 1993 and was replaced in the film by another young actor, Christian Slater, who donated his salary for the film to Phoenix's favorite charities, in his memory.

Interview with the Vampire

Kirsten's first feature role would have been a challenge for any actress, but considering that she was only ten years old when the filming of *Interview with the Vampire* began, her performance is even more impressive. The movie, based on the cult-classic novel by Anne Rice, tells the story of eighteenth-century Louisiana plantation owner Louis (played by Brad Pitt) who has lost his will to live after the death of his wife. He meets a creature called the Vampire Lestat (played by Tom Cruise) who offers him a different life as a vampire.

In the film, Kirsten played Claudia, an ageless vampire in the body of a little girl. She auditioned for the part along with five thousand other actresses, including Christina Ricci and Dominique Swain. But it was Dunst who brought tears to the eyes of casting director Joanna Colbert. There was violence in the film, as well as a scene that shocked some moviegoers in which Kirsten kissed thirty-year-old actor Brad Pitt. But Kirsten defends her choice to accept the role of Claudia, as well as her mother's decision to let her play the part. She told *Rolling Stone* magazine:

> My mom wouldn't have let me do the role if she thought there was something wrong with it. She knew how much I wanted that role because I knew it would set me off on my career. Besides, the blood and gore didn't bother me because I knew it was all fake. I think a less experienced young girl might have had a problem with it, but I didn't

feel there was anything wrong with me playing that role. Tom [Cruise] and Brad [Pitt] protected me throughout the whole movie. They treated me like a princess.[8]

But while her big-name costars treated her like a princess off camera, Kirsten had to be a professional when the cameras rolled. During the five months that the film was being made, she and Inez and Christian moved between New Orleans, Louisiana, and Paris, France. Moving was just one of the many challenges Kirsten faced in playing Claudia. She was forced to keep vampire hours on the set, as much of the filming was done between 4 P.M. and 2 A.M. Unlike the adult actors—Tom Cruise, Brad Pitt, Antonio Banderas, and Christian Slater—Kirsten also had to have an on-set tutor for three hours during the day to keep up with her schoolwork. She said it was sometimes tough to keep her eyes open while she was studying.

Kirsten also struggled with her period costumes—unwieldy hoopskirts and constrictive eighteenth-century corsets. "They were so tight that every time I ate or drank something I could feel it going down," she told *People* magazine after the film was released. "I wouldn't want to eat 'cause it felt so weird."[9]

One thing that was not weird for Kirsten was the fantasy aspect of the film. She understood that it was only make-believe and loved imagining she really was a little vampire. Although she was starring in a movie that would be considered scary (and

Kirsten Dunst and Hollywood's Leading Men

At just ten years old, Dunst was living the dream of girls everywhere—she was working alongside Hollywood "hunks" Brad Pitt, Tom Cruise, Antonio Banderas, and Christian Slater. But because she was just ten, their (sex) appeal was lost on her. But they made up for that in other ways. She told *People* magazine in 1994 that Cruise was cool because he got her tickets to a sold-out Janet Jackson concert; "Antonio Banderas is 'so loving—he'd always come in in the morning and give me a big hug.' And then there's Brad Pitt, whom she found 'hang-loose and fun'—until they sorta, almost, kinda had a kissing scene. 'I had to lean down and touch my lips to his,' says the actress. 'It was gross 'cause his lips were so dry.'" At the time, Kirsten thought the thirty-year-old Pitt had "cooties."

As a ten-year-old actress, Kirsten impressed her costars with her acting abilities during shooting of Interview with the Vampire.

off-limits, with an R-rating) for most kids her age, the film crew showed Kirsten what was happening behind the scenes so she was not traumatized by the heavy-duty horror film props. Special- effects expert Start Winston took Dunst around and said, "Here are the dead people, here's my mechanical rat." Says Kirsten, "It wasn't really scary, because you see all the fake stuff. It was like, 'Cut! Take out your [prosthetic vampire] teeth.'"[10]

Pint-Sized Actress

In addition to spending time with Winston, Kirsten spent hours working with an acting coach for the first time. She had never had formal training, and although she had natural talent, Kirsten benefited from his expertise, especially in learning to understand her character. She says: "He helped me understand, as best I could, what this little vampire girl was going through. I had to be sexual, but I also had to find the rage inside. Who knows how to do that when you're 10 years old? How do you relate? I had to find something to push those buttons. I'd go around slamming doors to get that rage."[11]

Kirsten won several awards for her work as Claudia in Interview with the Vampire, *including an MTV Movie Award in 1995.*

Not only did Kirsten find her rage, her experienced costars were amazed by her acting abilities. They would watch in disbelief as little Kirsten filmed her scenes. Tom Cruise told reporters: "We're all in awe of her maturity as an actress. There seems to be the experience of a 35-year-old actress in the body of this little girl."[12]

What few people knew at the time was that Kirsten understood her character in a strange way. She insisted that while she was filming the movie, she frequently felt the presence of ghosts. "They always wanted to communicate," she says. "And I'd get so scared that I'd have to ask them to leave me alone."[13]

Supernatural elements aside, *Interview with the Vampire* was a huge success, taking in more than $40 million in its opening weekend alone. The film was also an amazing experience for the young actress. Even as an adult, Kirsten said her favorite movie moment was on the last day on the set of *Interview with the Vampire*: "We were on the cobblestone streets of Paris at 3 A.M., the cast and crew toasted me with champagne, and I got a gold-and-diamond heart bracelet."[14] Even though she was too young to taste the champagne, Kirsten celebrated with her friends and got to feel the camaraderie that comes with getting to know the other actors and completing a project of which they were all proud.

Kirsten was praised for her performance, which Tom Gliatto and David Hiltbrand of *People* magazine called "touching and eerily funny."[15] Following the film's 1994 release, Kirsten was nominated for a Golden Globe Award for her work in the film and won the Boston Critics Society of Film Critics Award for Best Supporting Actress, the Chicago Film Critics Association Award for Most Promising Actress, the MTV Movie Award for Breakthrough Performance, and the YoungStar Award for Best Actress in a Drama. Suddenly, Kirsten was more than just another cute face on TV. She was an actress to be reckoned with.

Chapter 2

Teen Star

Kirsten was just ten years old when filming for *Interview with the Vampire* began; she was twelve and growing when it was released. No longer the eerily adorable little girl from the film, she was now a pretty preteen. The transition from child to teen can be a difficult time for young actors and actresses who want to keep working: They are too old for the cute child roles that got them noticed, but too young to play older teens who may be falling in love, going to college, or otherwise assuming more central roles in films. This is also a time in which many former child stars rebel, turning to alcohol and drugs in an attempt to mask their disappointment over career setbacks.

With nearly a decade of show business behind her, Kirsten had observed these types of pitfalls and was able to avoid them. She says she has never tried drugs, and she does not smoke. On the career front, Kirsten and Burton were able to find several age-appropriate roles for her in films such as *Jumanji* and *Wag the Dog*. Thus, capitalizing on her big break as a child actress, Kirsten continued with her acting career, enjoying her success and, eventually, learning from less satisfactory projects.

Little Woman

Kirsten's next movie was released just a month after *Interview with the Vampire*. She starred as a young Amy March in a new film version of the beloved children's classic *Little Women*.

Kirsten read the novel by nineteenth-century American writer Louisa May Alcott four times before auditioning for the part, and clearly her research paid off. She liked the family in the film, and especially admired Marmee (the mother, played by actress Susan Sarandon). Kirsten saw Marmee as a modern, almost feminist mother, well ahead of her time, who supported her daughters' individual paths to womanhood.

Little Women was another period piece, meaning more corsets and cumbersome costumes. But unlike Kirsten's character in *Interview*, Amy was a sweet, but sometimes spoiled, little girl from a loving and normal home. The film tells the tale of the four March sisters—Meg, Jo, Beth, and Amy—of Concord, Massachusetts. Their family falls on hard times during the Civil

Kirsten appears at the 1995 premiere of Interview with the Vampire, *looking like a mature preteen actress.*

Kirsten (center) portrayed the young Amy March in Little Women, *acting alongside such seasoned actresses as Winona Ryder (left) and Susan Sarandon (second from right).*

War after their father goes off to fight, but as they cope with difficult circumstances, they grow up and finally each begins her adult life.

Kirsten enjoyed working with a cast composed almost entirely of women. Just as she had been a little sister to her adult male colleagues in *Interview with the Vampire,* she reprised the role with the older actresses in *Little Women:* Trini Alvarado (Meg), Winona Ryder (Jo), Claire Danes (Beth), and Samantha Mathis (who played the older Amy). She developed strong relationships with these more experienced actresses and learned from watching them work.

Although it was the fourth film version adapted from the famous book, *Little Women* won praise from both critics and audiences alike and would become a Christmastime classic. Kirsten shone in the ensemble acting piece, holding her own with seasoned performers and proving that she was more than a one-hit wonder.

Jumanji, The Siege at Ruby Ridge, and *Mother Night*

Kirsten's next project was a contemporary piece, totally different than any she had done before. The thirteen-year-old actress starred with comedian Robin Williams in the 1995 holiday film *Jumanji*. The special effects–filled movie was loosely based on the award-winning children's picture book by Christopher Van Allsburg. It tells the story of two children who get sucked into their favorite board game and have to keep playing to get out. It was called a "funny-scary family flick."[16]

It may have been scary for some young viewers to see jungle animals rampaging all over a movie screen, but for Kirsten, the computer-generated and animatronic beasts only made her job more challenging. Since many of the special effects were added after filming was complete, she had to react to thin air. Much of her acting was done with nothing to play to but a blue screen. Acting with a blue screen is common in films with lots of

Pictured is a scene from the 1995 film Jumanji. *Kirsten faced the challenges of acting in front of a blue screen for the film, which was loaded with special effects.*

special effects or animation, but this was Kirsten's first experience with it. "It was hard to look surprised when a lion's supposed to jump at us, but all you see is a piece of tape on the wall where it's supposed to be,"[17] she told *Entertainment Weekly.*

With spectacular visual effects and a big star like Robin Williams in the lead, *Jumanji* drew in moviegoers. Kirsten was happy about the film's success but was clear that she did not want to ever be in her character's shoes. She told a reporter: "I used to play Candy Land all the time when I was a kid . . . but I'm not sure I'd want to live in it."[18]

Kirsten's next role was also a departure for her, and again, she would not have wanted to be in her character's place. In the 1996 television miniseries *The Siege at Ruby Ridge,* Kirsten played Sara Weaver, the daughter of a white separatist. The miniseries was inspired by real-life events involving a controversial 1992 government raid on the Idaho home of Randy Weaver, who was charged with possession of multiple sawed-off shotguns. The raid turned into a ten-day siege and resulted in the deaths of a U.S. marshall, a young neighbor, and Weaver, his wife, and his son (his daughter was spared). The incident created public outcry against the U.S. marshals who approved the raid.

Veteran actors Randy Quaid and Laura Dern played Kirsten's character's parents, Randy and Vicki Weaver. For her moving performance, Kirsten won her second YoungStar Award, this one for Young Actress in a TV Miniseries or Movie. In addition to her films, her television work was also getting noticed by critics.

For her next film, *Mother Night,* Kirsten was cast alongside another experienced actor, Nick Nolte. She played a young woman named Resi Noth, a famous German actress and wife of Howard J. Campbell Jr., an American spy. The movie, based on a book by Kurt Vonnegut Jr., tells the story of an American living in Germany during World War II who is recruited to spy for the United States. He assumes the cover role of an anti-Semitic news broadcaster and lives a double life that continues even after the war. When it was released in 1996, the film received positive reviews, and Kirsten's résumé was now packed with impressive credits—especially for such a young teenager.

Troubles at Home

Although Kirsten was enjoying success as an actress, her family life had been stressful: In 1995, Inez and Klaus Dunst decided to divorce after three years of separation. The decision was not an easy one to make, since the couple had been together for many years. They had been college sweethearts at Carnegie Mellon University, and with two children, they had tried very hard to make their relationship work. Although the decision was

Although Kirsten's career was very successful, her family life was troubled. After three years of separation, her parents divorced in 1995.

a difficult one, both Inez and Klaus thought it was for the best for themselves as well as Kirsten and Christian. (Despite the divorce, Klaus eventually moved to the Los Angeles area to be near his children.)

Kirsten has publicly agreed that the divorce was for the best. She knew her parents were not happy in their marriage, and after the long period of separation, she was not devastated by the split. Years later, she told *Rolling Stone* magazine:

> My mom and dad are the most opposite people. This isn't the opposites-attract type, either. This is, "How . . . did you ever get together, you two?" What's the point in staying married for the kids? I mean, really, you're just doing more damage being together and fighting all the time. I know I'd rather live with one parent, see the other and have them both be happy.[19]

One thing that did upset Kirsten, however, was the media's suggestion that her parents' divorce was the result of her success as an actress. Klaus Dunst was surprised that his daughter's acting "hobby" had turned into an impressive career, but he was happy for Kirsten and proud of her success. While Kirsten knew in her heart that the rumors were unjustified, it hurt her to read such speculation in magazines and newspapers. "I've read that my parents separated because of my career," she says. "But that's not true at all."[20]

What was true was although she was just a teenager, Kirsten was the major breadwinner for her mother and brother. But Kirsten was happy to do it. Although Klaus sent spousal and child support to cover their needs, by this time Kirsten's earnings far outstripped her father's. Her money supplemented the family's standard of living, which was comfortable but not extravagant. Kirsten put away plenty of her money for the future, but she did splurge occasionally. She later told *Rolling Stone*: "It doesn't bother me that I support my family. Of course, I do have some pressure on me, but we're very blessed with our lifestyle. The thing I'm proud of is that I don't feel like I've gotten here on an easy road. I come from this little town in New Jersey, and I'm proud to say that no one helped us."[21]

Kirsten's House

Kirsten's first big purchase, when her career began to bring financial success, was a nice house for her family: her mother, Inez, little brother, Christian, their four cats, and a Yorkshire terrier named Beauty. *InStyle* magazine visited Kirsten and her family in their Toluca Lake home, complete with pool and updated kitchen with a '50s-style breakfast nook. According to Kirsten, "Everyone says we have the party house." But Kirsten likes being in the kitchen as much as partying by the pool. "If I weren't an actress," Kirsten says, "I'd want to be a chef."

Some of the proceeds from Kirsten's movie career went to buy a three-bedroom ranch home in the Toluca Lake section of Los Angeles, which Inez filled with furniture from the old house in New Jersey, as well as some new items from the flea markets and antique stores that she and Kirsten liked to frequent. They had found their dream house, and Kirsten was ready to put down roots in a new hometown.

Hits and Misses

Kirsten enrolled at Notre Dame High School, a private Catholic high school in Los Angeles, but she was so busy working that she got most of her schooling from tutors. During her sophomore year of high school in 1997 and 1998, she made three films and two made-for-television movies, did voiceovers in three different animated films, and had a recurring role on a popular television series.

Kirsten's big-screen film work included *True Heart*, in which she played a girl who is stranded along with her brother in the Canadian wilderness after a plane crash. Kirsten's costar was TV's *Home Improvement* heartthrob Zachery Ty Bryan. But the appeal of the film's two young stars was not enough to make the film a success, and it went straight to video.

Kirsten next starred in *Strike*, which was also called *All I Wanna Do*, a comedy set in 1963. When the pupils at an all-girls school find out that they are supposed to merge with a boys' school, they work together to prevent it from happening. The best part about making the movie for Kirsten was working with so many other young actresses, including Gaby Hoffmann, Monica Keena, Rachael Leigh Cook, and Heather Matarazzo, who became one of Kirsten's closest friends. But the film itself was forgettable.

Back on the Road to Success

After *True Heart* and *Strike* flopped, Kirsten was happy that her follow-up movie, *Wag the Dog*, starring acclaimed actors Robert De Niro and Dustin Hoffman, was well received. In *Wag the Dog*, De Niro plays a political spin doctor and Hoffman is a Hollywood director hired to divert attention from a presidential scan-

Kirsten appears at the 1997 premiere of Wag the Dog *with Dustin Hoffman and his son. The movie was a critical success.*

Life in the Spotlight

In the 1990s Dunst was one of the most famous and recognizable teen stars, but her days and nights were much like those of other teenagers. She did not go club hopping, eat at famous restaurants, or shop at high-end boutiques. She did go to parties at friends' houses, visit the food court of the local mall for a Mrs. Fields cookie, or shop at Rampage.

Teen stars of today, such as Lindsay Lohan, are often photographed drinking and dancing or buying expensive clothes and designer handbags. Some appear in magazines in provocative, sexy poses. Dunst says she is concerned for these young stars. She wishes they could have the relatively normal life she had as a young star.

dal by creating a fictitious war. Kirsten's role in the film was small but memorable. She played a young actress named Tracy Lime, who is hired to play a refugee in a fake war scene that is going to be shown on television. In addition to the political parody, it was fun for Kirsten to poke fun at the Hollywood world of acting. Oblivious to the gigantic fraud in which she is participating, her character pesters the crew about whether she will get credit on the piece, whether she will be able to put it on her résumé, and so on.

Filming *Wag the Dog* was memorable for Kirsten in more ways than one. On the set, she met a young man close to her own age, Dustin Hoffman's son, Jake Hoffman, and there were rumors that she briefly dated him.

Fifteen and Working

No less important and notable than Kirsten's movie work were her television credits. She was cast alongside Steve Guttenberg and Nia Peeples in the Disney TV thriller *Tower of Terror*. Kirsten also landed a coveted recurring role on the hit NBC drama *ER*. She played Charlene (Charlie) Chiemengo, a troubled runaway teen who is befriended by Dr. Doug Ross, played by George Clooney.

Kirsten's next role was as a troubled young girl who discovers she is pregnant at age fifteen. Made for television, *Fifteen and Pregnant* was based on the true story of young Tina Spangler and the choices she faced after learning she was pregnant. Although

In addition to acting in movies, Kirsten kept herself busy with television work, including a recurring role on the hit drama ER *(cast pictured).*

she decided to have the baby, she was not allowed to attend regular high school. Her parents struggled with her decision and her boyfriend broke up with her, leaving her a single teen mother.

Kirsten earned critical praise for her work on the movie and won her third consecutive YoungStar Award courtesy of the *Hollywood Reporter.* But even more meaningful to Kirsten was the fan mail she received after playing the role. She knew that teen pregnancy rates were high, but reading the personal and touching stories of girls her own age who were raising children was an eye-opening experience for the actress. She told *Teen People* magazine: "I got so much mail after that movie aired. Girls [were] telling me about their own experiences. It was just amazing."[22]

In addition to making movies and television appearances, Kirsten did voiceovers for several animated films, including *The Animated Adventures of Tom Sawyer*, *Small Soldiers*, and Disney's *Anastasia.* It was fun and interesting for Kirsten to mix up her regular acting with something a little different. Plus, she got to work with some big stars—including Meg Ryan, Kelsey Grammer, John Cusack, and Christopher Lloyd—on these projects.

High School Days

With all the work she was doing, it was hard for Kirsten to have a normal high school experience. Thanks to the combination of tutoring and classroom studying, however, Kirsten received mostly As and Bs in her classes at Notre Dame High School. And even though she was not in class every day, she attended as many school events as possible and she had lots of friends to socialize with when she was not working. Kirsten liked having

In this photo, Kirsten poses with Kelsey Grammer and a character from Anastasia, *one of several animated films for which the young actress did voiceover work.*

friends who were not in show business to take her mind off of work just as much as she liked having a few good actress friends who understood the ups and downs of the business.

Looking back on her high school career, Kirsten has fond memories. She once even flew back to Los Angeles in the midst of an out-of-town job for a dance she didn't want to miss. "I went to football games," she recalls, "and I was a cheerleader and I was really nice to everybody because I would have been a really easy target [for teasing]."[23] With her career and good looks, Kirsten knew that some people were envious and talked about her behind her back. She had experienced this even as a little girl in New Jersey. But she chose to ignore the negativity and go out of her way to be friendly to everyone. Kirsten's friends and family were her support system, and she was grateful to have them as her career took off.

Valuable though her high school years were, however, Kirsten admits that much of the time when she was studying, she was anxious to be back on the set. All the over-eighteen actors and actresses could chat and read magazines while waiting for the next shot to be set up, and Dunst looked forward to the day when she would not have to study on set. And those days were quickly approaching.

Chapter 3

Independent Spirit

D UNST WAS GROWING up, but she was still content to act her age and to play characters her age in movies. While many child and teen stars struggle to find roles as young adults and go through an awkward phase, Dunst seemed to make the transition seamlessly. For this, she was thankful. It kept her working and happy. Thanks to the guidance of her family and friends as well as her own good sense, she was able to avoid the pitfalls of drinking and drugs that many young actors and actresses encounter because of all the parties and events they attend. Instead, she was happy with simply working nonstop, going to high school functions, and spending time at home with her family and friends.

During her junior year of high school, Dunst starred in one made-for-cable movie and three big-screen films, including one that was completely different from any role she had ever played and would prove to be her second big break.

The Devil's Arithmetic

As some actors and actresses attain stardom, they stop accepting television and do only only big-screen films. Many more, however, remain open to the opportunities presented by a compelling role in a popular television series or made-for-television movie. Dunst, who had gotten her start in TV, did not disdain the small screen. She wanted to act in interesting projects, and when she was offered the lead in the 1999 Showtime drama *The Devil's Arithmetic*, she was happy to sign on; it was one of the best scripts she had ever read.

The Devil's Arithmetic tells the story of a young Jewish girl named Hannah Stern (played by Dunst). To the dismay of her family, Hannah does not embrace the Jewish traditions and knows little about the horrors of the Holocaust until she is asked to "open the front door" at her family's Seder feast. The Seder feast is a part of the important Jewish holiday of Passover, celebrated in late March or early April. *Seder* means "order," and there is a particular order to the Seder feast that includes opening the front door to symbolize welcoming the prophet Elijah into the home.

When she opens the front door for Elijah, Hannah is suddenly transported back in time to the 1940s, where she becomes a prisoner at a German concentration camp and is forced to live out the horrifying events her grandmother witnessed.

The film received positive reviews, and making it was instructive for Dunst, a Christian who was attending a Catholic school. Like her character, she knew little about Jewish culture and was very moved by what she learned about this traumatic and important time in world history.

A Return to Comedy

After the emotionally draining role of Hannah Stern, Dunst turned to two fluffy comedies. The sixteen-year-old actress's comedic talents, first seen on film in *Wag the Dog*, were put to use in *Drop Dead Gorgeous*, a beauty pageant parody released in 1999. Dunst played Amber Atkins, a small-town beauty pageant winner who wants to escape her humble background in tiny Mount Rose, Minnesota, and sees the Miss Teen Princess America pageant as her ticket out.

Standing in Amber's way is her alcoholic mother, played by Ellen Barkin, as well as another mother-daughter duo: a beautiful and rich contestant, played by Denise Richards, and her conniving mother, herself a former Miss Teen Princess America, played by Kirstie Alley. The film, which unfolds in mock documentary style, was shot in small towns all over Minnesota.

Audiences found the film amusing, as did Dunst. "It was absolutely the funniest script I've ever read," she told the *Orange County Register.* "I never gave much thought to beauty pageants before this, but this film is about so much more than beauty pageants."[24] Instead it was about winning at all costs and the de-

After taking on a series of serious roles, Dunst (center) returned to comedy with the part of Amber in the 1999 film Drop Dead Gorgeous.

sire for fame. Many actresses could probably understand the competitive and cutthroat atmosphere of beauty pageants as well.

Dunst had been in Hollywood long enough to the see the parallels as well. Although she was a successful actress, who liked to practice her craft at every opportunity, at other times, she wanted to live a normal life among family and friends with varied interests. She even liked living some distance from Hollywood, where many show business celebrities like to live.

It was her refreshing honesty and amazing normalcy that had made the film's director, Michael Patrick Jann, want Dunst for the role of Amber. Jann did not care about her impressive list of credits or notice her work in a particular movie. Instead, it was Dunst being herself on an episode of television's *Teen Jeopardy* that convinced him she was right for the role. He explains:

> She was standing there on the panel between two obnoxious sitcom kids who were trying desperately to act smart and cool. But Kirsten wasn't trying to pretend she

Dunst (second from left) smiles at the premiere of Drop Dead Gorgeous *with costars Brittany Murphy, Amy Adams, and Denise Richards.*

was anything except what she was. She radiated genuineness. Every emotion was right there on her face; I found myself charmed watching her on that show. She was a total natural, which is refreshing in Hollywood. There is such a shortage of that in young actors. They are all aspiring to be Al Pacino and they think every film has to be "The Godfather." None of them want to work at their craft and build a career. Kirsten is a total pro, but she hasn't lost her innocence. There is a real intelligence about her, but she still acts like a teen-age girl. You can talk to her about the complexities of a scene one moment, and the next moment she's talking about the Spice Girls, and she talks about both with the same enthusiasm. She's the real deal.[25]

Another Comedy

For her next comedic role, in the movie *Dick*, Dunst played young Betsy Jobs, who becomes the president's official dog walker after meeting President Richard Nixon on a school field trip. In this completely fictitious script, Betsy and her friend Arlene (played by actress Michelle Williams) unintentionally witness both the break-in at the Watergate Hotel and the coverup of the Watergate scandal, and unwittingly become the "deep throats" (inside sources) providing information to Bob Woodward

Continuing to showcase her comedic skills, Dunst (right) appeared in Dick *as Betsy Jobs, a woman who becomes President Richard Nixon's dog walker.*

and Carl Bernstein, the *Washington Post* reporters who covered the story in real life. Before shooting the film, Dunst knew little about the Watergate affair, which had been front-page news a decade before her birth. Again, however, Dunst learned a lot about history, even though no such character as Betsy Jobs had figured into the actual events.

Dunst had fun making the film, especially enjoying the wardrobe and the roller-skating scenes. Her favorite outfit consisted of blue short shorts with white stars, a red-and-white striped halter top, and a big floppy hat with a yellow smiley face.

Pretending to be a teen in the Nixon years gave Dunst a chance to act goofy in and around Washington, D.C. One of the most popular pastimes of the time was roller-skating, which has since been replaced by rollerblading. For the film, Dunst had to learn how to roller-skate in bell bottom pants, which was not easy. Each roller-skating scene required many takes to get it right, and audiences never saw the wobbles and falls Dunst and Williams took as they acquired the new skill.

With the release of *Drop Dead Gorgeous* and *Dick* in the summer of 1999, Dunst was proving that she was a skilled comedienne, but she was ready for yet another kind of challenge.

"Smart, Sexy, and Sad"

"Obviously, the roles I get offered all the time are that of the nice blonde," Dunst told an interviewer in 1999. "But I don't want to go in that direction. I am also starting to get offered the sexy roles, but that doesn't interest me much, either. I always wanted to play a psycho killer."[26] Although her next role was not that of a murderer, Dunst did play against type in a film about five teenage sisters in the fictional Lisbon family. The girls are raised in a very strict and religious family that forbids the sisters to date, socialize, or even go to school after Lux (Dunst's character) breaks curfew. The youngest daughter commits suicide in one of the movie's early scenes, and by the end of the film, *The Virgin Suicides*, the four older siblings have followed suit.

The Virgin Suicides was the first feature film of Academy Award–winning director and writer Sofia Coppola, then known

Kirsten's Friendships

In May of 2002, Kirsten told *Scholastic Choices* magazine all about her friendships.

Choices: As a teen, did you have many friends?

Kirsten: In middle school, my friend Molly would defend me if anyone said bad things about me. In high school, I made other friends, like my friend Cindy. They've all been good to me. I've found that the best friends support you and don't get jealous because they have their own interests.

Choices: Are you close with other actors?

Kirsten: Not really. I'm friends with Brittany Murphy and I see her once a year. I'm probably closest to Heather Matarazzo.

Choices: How do you handle people who latch on to you because you're famous?

Kirsten: You can tell when people want to be friends for ulterior reasons. You have to feel the situation out and stop hanging out with those people because it's bad.

mainly as the daughter of renowned director Francis Ford Coppola of *The Godfather* movies. In casting her debut film, based on the book by Jeffrey Eugenides, Coppola wanted Dunst to play Lux, the most desirable and rebellious of the girls. Dunst was thrilled that someone saw her as more than the "happy, cute, perky Kirsten. . . . [Coppola] wanted me to be smart, sexy, and sad. All things I was but that nobody else ever wanted me to show."[27]

Dunst enjoyed working with Coppola and enjoyed her interpretation of the script as well as her direction. Coppola was equally impressed with Dunst, whom she saw as a serious actress and goofy teenager rolled into one. She explained to *In-Style* magazine that other actresses are "15 going on 40. They've been emancipated since they were 9. But Kirsten is innocent despite being a very mature actress."[28]

Critics and audiences alike were happy that Dunst had been called on to show off this new side of herself. Dunst got some of the best reviews of her twenty-five-film career. *Rolling Stone* called her "wonderfully funny and touching."[29] Another reporter

said: "Dunst captures the luminescence of the Lisbon sisters, ex-
uding sensuality and mystery, and always somehow forbid-
den."[30] And Glen Lovell of the *San Jose Mercury News* said: "The
16-year-old Dunst (*Dick, Drop Dead Gorgeous*) keeps getting better with every movie. Her Lux is a lot more than a countercul-
ture Lolita; she's sexy, smoldering and smart."[31]

Indie Film Provides Dunst's Second Big Break

The Virgin Suicides was Dunst's first independent film, which
means that it was made without the backing of a large Hollywood
studio. Independent films, or indies, are often very creative,
being less reliant on visual effects and big-name stars than films
from the major studios, and they are considered to be riskier at
the box office. When they do succeed, as *The Virgin Suicides* did,
they can make a huge return on profits because they do not cost
very much to make. After three years of playing variations on
the same character, starring in *The Virgin Suicides* was Dunst's second big break in the wake of *Interview with the Vampire*.

Before appearing in Coppola's film, Dunst had begun to be
concerned that her triumphant debut in *Interview with the Vampire*
represented a peak she might not achieve again. She had been
working steadily for the past eight years, but none of her roles or
movies had been as exciting as Lux in *The Virgin Suicides*.

The film was more than just great material and characters,
however. With *The Virgin Suicides*, Dunst rediscovered one of the
things she loved about acting–connecting with the people she
worked with, especially the girls who played her sisters. She and
the other young actresses lunched together and drew pictures
during filming breaks in Dunst's trailer. She made a collage of
all their artwork and hung it on her trailer's window. Dunst also
enjoyed working with James Woods and Kathleen Turner, the
veteran actors cast to play the five girls' parents. She explains in
an interview on the movie's official Web site: "[T]here was such
a family atmosphere on the set and it so rarely happens that it's
such a magical feeling when you're filming."[32]

Much of the acting in the film made use of body language
rather than dialogue, creating a new challenge for Dunst: "That's
one of the reasons I chose this film was because a lot of it is

Dunst poses at the 2000 premiere of The Virgin Suicides, *her first independent film. Critics praised her dynamic performance in the film.*

about human behavior. . . . It's so much more challenging to express your emotions without the words. Sometimes words get in the way almost,"[33] she explains. Dunst's performance in the film was perhaps the most talked about of the year. She felt revitalized and happy with her work.

Class of 2000

Dunst was excited that her career was on the upswing as she was
about to graduate from high school. Since acting was her cho-
sen profession and she had been doing it for more than a
decade, she had no doubts about the career she would pursue.
While her friends left for colleges in Colorado and Arizona, she
stayed in Los Angeles. Although it was admittedly hard for her

Director Sofia Coppola and Dunst are pictured at the New York City premiere of The Virgin Suicides.

to watch her friends leave and go on to school, Dunst knew she would take classes again someday in writing or Spanish.

Dunst was aware that she might well be admitted to an Ivy League school simply because she was a famous actress. "My grades weren't straight As," she told an interviewer, "but if I wanted to go to Columbia, they would probably just let me in and justify it by saying 'Oh, but she's so dedicated to her work.'"[34]

So instead of moving into a dorm room, Dunst and her mom set about renovating their home, adding more space for her now that she was a full-fledged adult. They added an elaborate loft to give her more privacy. Dunst admitted that she was glad to still be home and have her family, with whom she is very close, nearby. Some people wondered why she did not move out and get her own place right away. Dunst knew that living on her own was still a couple of years away, and she defended her decision to live at home for a little while longer. "Why do people think that it's weird for me to be living with my mom? I'm 18. It's not like I'm 30,"[35] she said.

Although she was years away from thirty, Dunst had a career that was the envy of many actresses twice her age. And it showed no signs of slowing.

Chapter 4

Breaking the Mold

W HEN MOST OF her girlfriends were entering college, Dunst was in the middle of her working career, making back-to-back films; but even though she was out of high school in real life, she starred in *Bring It On* and the musical comedy *Get Over It*, bringing both believability and mature insight to roles as high school girls. Dunst was not much older than the characters she was playing, and she understood what each was going through.

But the momentum her career had gained after the release of *The Virgin Suicides* was soon dissipated by such mediocre movies like *Deeply*, *Luckytown*, *All Forgotten*, and *The Crow: Salvation*. Dunst, however, was working at a breakneck pace and failed to realize she was in a rut until she approached the end of her teens. The projects she took on seemed interesting and worthwhile at the time, and even Inez and Dunst's agent, Iris Burton, thought she was making the right choice in taking the roles. It was only later that they regretted their decisions. Dunst renewed her vow to work on fewer projects, emphasizing quality over quantity. The next film she chose, *crazy/beautiful*, would give her one of her most daring and different roles to date.

Bring It On

Dunst had been a cheerleader in high school—when she could make games and practices, that is—so she knew a little something about playing her next character, Torrance (Tor) Shipman, in the comedy *Bring It On*. In the movie, Tor is selected as the new captain of the cheerleading squad and entrusted with the task of leading the Rancho Carne Torros to their fourth win at the National Cheerleading Championships. Victory seems within their grasp, but a twist in the plot forces Tor to abandon cheers the squad has used successfully for years and create new routines just weeks before the championship. The film's director, Peyton Reed, called it "an affectionate look at the world of cheerleading, in all its competitive and catty glory."[36]

Even though she had some cheerleading experience, Dunst and the other actresses cast as her squad mates went to an intense cheerleading camp to learn and perfect their moves. The result was worth the effort. In all but one scene in the movie (featuring actress Eliza Dushku) the cheerleaders' moves were performed by the actors themselves.

Reviews for *Bring It On* were mixed. Steve Rea of the *Philadelphia Inquirer* compared Dunst's performance to that of actress Reese Witherspoon in the acclaimed 1999 movie *Election.*

As a former cheerleader, Dunst brought a degree of authenticity to her role as a cheerleader in the 2000 film Bring It On.

Rea said the film itself was a "likable, low-budget high school comedy" that "as fluffy, adolescent fantasy [was] better than most."[37] However, reviewer Devin Rose of the *Chicago Tribune* said that the film put the "ugh in ugly."[38] However, the film was popular with young audiences, and it boosted Dunst's appeal with teen moviegoers.

Feeling Uninspired

After having fun making the high school cheerleader comedy, Dunst set to work on a string of projects that were less enjoyable for her to make and for moviegoers to see: *The Crow: The Salvation*, *Luckytown*, *Deeply*, and *All Forgotten*. Dunst suggests that staying busy on these lackluster projects served to divert her from even less pleasant, but unspecified, aspects of her personal life. A few years later, she candidly told *Teen Vogue*: "I was so uninspired. I'd be like, 'When are we going to wrap? What time is lunch?'"[39]

In *The Crow: The Salvation*, the third installment of an action film series, Dunst played Erin Randall, whose sister has been murdered. Some reviews for the film were more favorable than others, but the project did little to enhance Dunst's career.

In *Luckytown*, Dunst played a girl named Lidda Daniels who travels to Las Vegas from Southern California to find her professional gambler father, who had abandoned her years before. *Deeply* was based on the premise that a good story has the power to heal. In the film, a traumatized teen meets a writer who tells her the story of another troubled teen named Silly (played by Dunst). *All Forgotten*, set in nineteenth-century Russia, is the story of a young man who falls in love with a coquette.

After these unsatisfying moviemaking experiences, Dunst made an important decision. She decided to work a lot less, but on movies she cared about a lot more. In short, she decided to follow her initial instincts about a project and turn down any that did not strike her as different and interesting from the start. "Playing it smart is just following your intuition," says Dunst. "I've done movies that I haven't followed my gut on, and it turned out I didn't enjoy the movie in the end or something wasn't right."[40]

Dunst arrives at the premiere of Bring It On. *The movie bolstered the actress's appeal with younger audiences.*

Kirsten's Most Beautiful

Kirsten has been receiving awards for her acting since her big break in *Interview with the Vampire*. She was a three-time recipient of the YoungStar Award as well as a frequent face on *People* magazine's annual Most Beautiful People list. In 2002, the twenty-year-old made their list with a picture and write-up:

"No matter how tired I am, I always wash my face at the end of the day," she says. The 5'5" actress insists she eats properly and doesn't need "to run on a treadmill or do any of that creepy stuff." Evidently her natural exuberance is a great conditioner—for herself and others. "She gives you a positive charge," says Spider-Man director Sam Raimi. "It's the Dunst charge." Adds her costar Willem Defoe: "She's a little ball of fire who can hold her own against actors much more her senior."

Dunst was so comfortable financially that she could afford to be choosy. Now her focus was more on being happy with her life than on having a successful career. "I want to be happy in the scene I'm working in," She explained in 2003. "I'm learning that you still have to live your life–if you don't, you can't be a good actress."[41] Dunst's vow to make fewer, higher-quality projects paid off with her next two projects, the musical comedy *Get Over It* and the romantic drama *crazy/beautiful*.

Romance on the Set

Get Over It tells the story of Berke (played by Ben Foster), a young man who is dumped by his girlfriend, Allison, and decides to get a part in the school play to win her back. Instead, he ends up falling for a friend's younger sister, Kelly (played by Dunst). Dunst explains that Kelly is Berke's shoulder to cry on until he realizes that she is more than just a friend.

Before making *Get Over It*, Dust had made it a rule not to date her costars, even though she had worked with some of the hottest young actors in the business, such as Josh Hartnett in *The Virgin Suicides*. She did not take whatever crushes she formed while filming too seriously until she met Ben Foster, her costar in *Get Over It*. The two began dating, and Foster was the first boyfriend Dunst publicly acknowledged. She told *Cosmopolitan* magazine in April 2001:

Sometimes when you're working on a film, a guy gets to you. Maybe you'll get a little crush, but you know what? After the film, you usually realize that you can't have a conversation with him about anything other than what happened on the set. I never go for the hot guys anyway. They're always the ones who break your heart. In general, I still don't think it's a very good idea to get involved with your costars. But actors are only human. If sparks fly, they fly. This is the first time I've had a boyfriend while I was promoting a film. I don't want to talk about him too much in articles and have him start to get weirded out about it. I'm only 18. By the time this article comes out, things could be different.[42]

And things were different even before the film was released. Dunst and Foster, who had stopped seeing each other, were called back to the set for a reshoot of a romantic scene. This

When Dunst fell for Ben Foster on the set of Get Over It *in 2001, she broke her own rule about not dating costars.*

meant that they had to put aside any negative feelings about the breakup and act as though they were in love. They proved to be good actors. Later, fans were surprised to learn that the actors were not dating when the scene was filmed. Dunst cried over Foster but then moved on. She had too much to be happy about to let the breakup bring her down for long.

Thus, the breakup did not sour Dunst's good feelings about making *Get Over It*, which also starred musical star Sisqo and Tom Hanks's son Colin. Dunst found her costars amusing and enjoyed filming in Toronto, Ontario, Canada, a popular and inexpensive location for filming outside of Hollywood. The young cast would go out to eat and go dancing in the evenings. They sometimes bumped into superstars such as Jennifer Lopez, which still awed Dunst even though she was now well on the way to becoming a celebrity herself.

The film also included Dunst's first foray into singing on screen. Some moviegoers doubted whether it was really Dunst flexing her vocal cords, but it was not a voice double. "That's me!" Dunst says. "It's the first time I've sung on camera because I'm shy."[43] Dunst overcame her shyness and did not only the lip-synching for the camera but also sang on the soundtrack. There were even rumors of a recording contract, but Dunst has not been in a recording studio since.

Playing Against Type

Although her singing had people talking, Dunst was content to focus on acting for now. And for good reason: Her acting was definitely receiving attention. With the release of *crazy/beautiful* in 2000, Dunst also broke free from her previous bubbly, all-American-girl image. The film was a big risk for Kirsten, because her character was not as likable or innocent as those she had become known for playing. In the film, her character, Nicole Oakley, is a wealthy, depressed teen who falls in love with Carlos Nuñez, a poor Hispanic boy. The two struggle to make their relationship work despite their vastly different backgrounds and disapproval from family and friends on both sides.

Dunst was drawn to the script for the film because although her character was a teenager, it was definitely not a typical teen

Dunst, shown here with costar Jay Hernandez, shed her wholesome image when she accepted the role of the dysfunctional Nicole in crazy/beautiful.

movie. She was holding to her decision to move away from the fluffy, predictable type of film that targets preteen audiences.

In another departure from type, her character in *crazy/beautiful* was not the beautiful one—she was crazy, as Carlos tells her in the film. Nicole is the bad girl, while her love interest is the studious, motivated young man whom she calls "beautiful." Although some around her were concerned that she would be forever shattering her image as the wholesome girl-next-door by taking the part, Dunst was more than ready to show that she could project qualities other than "cute" and "sweet."

Once filming began, Dunst was so convincing as the strung-out Nicole that studio executives wondered if she was using drugs, like her character. Director John Stockwell said: "Before I would say, 'Action,' she'd be Kiki—perky and bright-eyed. Then cameras would roll, her eyes would glaze over, and her voice would change. She became this moody, depressed, dysfunctional girl."[44]

It was hard on Dunst, who was not used to feeling like this character. It is Dunst's nature to want to feel good about life, while Nicole seemed determined to only feel bad. "This movie made me feel like crap every day," Dunst told *Rolling Stone* magazine. "It's hard to get to certain places, like being drunk and doing drugs. I can't say I've never had a drink before, but I've never actually done a drug in my life."[45]

To help her get into character, Dunst had to find things that made her feel moody and depressed. Reading the poems of writer Sylvia Plath helped (the depressive young mother committed suicide in 1963); so did listening to lyrics from Joni Mitchell's *Blue*. But Dunst did not have to wonder about where her character was coming from on one issue: love. Still in the early days of her relationship with Foster, she had this in com-

Roles Not Taken

Hollywood is a competitive place—even for a respected actress like Kirsten. What few moviegoers realize when they see a movie is that the actors and actresses in the roles are rarely ever the ones first offered those parts. Kirsten has both lost out on roles she wanted to other talented young actresses and turned certain parts down for various reasons.

Kirsten turned down a role in 1995's *Now & Then*. It was reported that she did not want to have to gain weight to play the part of young Chrissy. She also said no to Mena Suvari's memorable role as a teenage temptress in 1999's *American Beauty*. She explained to zap2it.com: "When I read [the script], I was 15 and I don't think I was mature enough to understand the script's material. I didn't want to be kissing Kevin Spacey. Come on! Lying there naked with rose petals?" Kirsten also passed on playing the title role in the 2003 film *Girl with a Pearl Earring* because of scheduling conflicts. Actress Kate Hudson turned down the role as well, and actress Scarlett Johanssen eventually played the part.

mon with Nicole. Explains Dunst, "The character is falling in love for the first time, and I was going through that, too."[46]

The movie was more real than the typical teen flick, and it handled drinking, drug use, and sex among teens with honesty. According to the director: "It was a little more honest and open before the [Motion Picture Association of America] ratings board got their hands on it."[47] Disney, the studio backing the film, wanted it to be more family friendly and asked Stockwell for editing changes that would result in a PG-13 rating. The end result was a film that does not show Nicole smoking marijuana; additionally, some of the profanity was removed and the sex scenes were shortened, but not removed entirely.

First Adult Love Scene

Dunst is a little skeptical about nudity in her films because she thinks it is tasteless and interferes with her wish to be a good role model for young girls. Thus her character in *crazy/beautiful* never appears completely nude. The film does, however, contain Dunst's first sex scene, and she emphasizes that the level at which the sex scene was played was the choice of the director: "[Nudity] was in the script, but I would never do that and they knew that. I don't think it's necessary. The script was much more wholesome and sweet [at the start of shooting]. It's funny, I'm surprised that the studio even let us go where we did. But that's what I knew John Stockwell wanted to do."[48]

Stockwell himself was not always sure that Dunst could convincingly play the scene because he thought that she was perhaps too innocent and naive. "I'd read that she was a virgin. I left with some uncertainty that she could pull off the role of a sexual provocateur,"[49] he recalls.

His doubts, however, were soon put to rest. Stockwell learned that Dunst was an actress with enough range to play roles of many different types, regardless of whether she had personally had the same experiences as her character.

Stockwell was impressed with Dunst's attitude as well as her performance during the filming of the sex scene. She was not particularly self-conscious, but instead very professional and businesslike. "She wasn't pulling up the sheet or asking 'Is my ass showing?'" Stockwell says. "This woman, who can come off so prim and proper, turned out to be more than able to adopt the attitude of a girl who takes control. People who are expecting the Kirsten from *Bring It On* are going to be in for a big shock."[50]

Dunst was surprisingly comfortable doing the sex scene, but she did not find it as romantic and sexual as her character did. She recalled to *Cosmopolitan* magazine: "I had these little pasties over my boobs—it was horrible. My costar, Jay Hernandez, was so uncomfortable about doing the scene that his nervousness actually made it easier for me to handle."[51] She ended up placing Hernandez's hand on her breast and jokingly telling him that it would not bite. The joke broke the ice, and the awkwardness was gone. The result was a convincing love scene.

After *crazy/beautiful*

After filming, Dunst and her mother decided to watch the sex scene together, which proved to be a little uncomfortable for them both. Inez was somewhat surprised by her daughter's performance, but Kirsten, who does not like to discuss sex or whether she is sexually active, would not comment on any prior experience she may have brought to the role. However, Dunst was proud of her performance and of the film itself.

The film was a hit, especially with younger audiences, who liked the storyline of a romance between the rich white girl who is a rebellious troublemaker and the poor Hispanic boy who is determined to live a good life despite not being able to afford to go to college. Moreover, Nicole's father wants Carlos to stop seeing Nicole, stating that she is a bad influence on the serious young man. He sees potential in the underprivileged youth, but, sadly, none in his own daughter. "The young audience is much more color-blind than their parents," says MTV Productions president Van Toffler, discussing the film's appeal. "It's reflected in the television they watch and the music they listen to."[52]

Critics were equally impressed. Steven Rea of the *Philadelphia Inquirer* called it "an intelligent romance that cuts against the grain of the youth-pic genre, *crazy/beautiful* boasts a scarily good performance from Dunst as Nicole Oakley, a self-destructive rich kid whose favorite pastime is getting wasted. . . . *crazy/beautiful*

Taryn Manning poses with Dunst at the Hollywood premiere of crazy/beautiful. *The two played best friends in the hit movie.*

feels right; and its two stars, Hernandez and Dunst, spark off of each other. You believe he's ready to throw it all away for her, and that she's capable—and, worthy—of being saved by him."[53] And Dave Willoughby of the *Times* in the United Kingdom called it: "superior teen fare."[54]

Thanks to her careful decisions and hard work, Dunst was officially out of her career rut, and she had no intention of ever going back.

Chapter 5

The Big Time

As SHE APPROACHED the end of her teen years, well launched on a successful acting career, Dunst decided it was time to be on her own. Even though she was extremely close to her mother, she wanted a space of her own, separate from her beloved loft suite in the house in Toluca Lake. It was exciting for Dunst to have her own home to decorate and her own space in which to entertain friends.

To go along with her new home, Dunst had a new role—the biggest of her career. She beat out hundreds of young actresses to play the love interest of Peter Parker, aka Spider-Man. *crazy/beautiful* director Stockwell was not surprised that the business-savvy Dunst nabbed the prestigious role. He told *Cosmopolitan*: "She is so mature and aware of how the business works."[55]

The Cat's Meow

The role of the superhero's girlfriend was not Dunst's first adult role. In 2001 she starred as silent film star Marion Davies in director Peter Bogdanovich's period piece *The Cat's Meow*. Set in November 1924, the film is based on a true story and the plot revolves around a mysterious death aboard a yacht owned by media mogul William Randolph Hearst. In the film, Marion has a relationship with Hearst as well as one with fellow actor Charlie Chaplin.

Once again, Dunst was filmed kissing someone more than twice her age. This time, however, her kiss went not to super-hunk Brad Pitt, but to fifty-something character actor Edward Hermann. She told E!Online: "Ed has a daughter my age; it was really creepy to think about. I was like, Okay, pretend you're kissing your dad goodbye or something."[56]

Her portrayal of Davies, one of America's first superstars, was so convincing that Dunst won the 2002 Argentinian Mar del Plata International Film Festival Award for Best Actress. Her performance in the April 2002 release also won critical praise (although the movie itself garnered mixed reviews). Tom Carson of *Esquire* magazine, who called Dunst's performance "terrific," went on to describe her big scene in the film:

> Chaplin does most of the talking. Yet you barely notice his frantic spiel; you're mesmerized by Dunst's reactions. She's playing a likable, carefree woman who prides

Marion Davies was a superstar of the silent film era in the 1920s. In 2001 Dunst played Davies in The Cat's Meow.

herself on not being calculating. But now she's thinking
fast, and you watch her figure out that taking a chance
on love is one thing but swapping a megalomaniac who
dotes on her for an unreliable narcissist is another. As
she does, her character's unreflective face grows so elo-
quent that Davies's decision goes on making sense even

Dunst, here at the premiere for The Cat's Meow, *won critical acclaim
for her portrayal of Marion Davies.*

after the murderous denouement. . . . One reason it seems appropriate for Dunst to play a silent star in *The Cat's Meow* is that she's got a seemingly unaffected gift for making unarticulated emotions photographable.[57]

Getting the Part

As memorable as her performance in *The Cat's Meow* was, the role almost cost her an arguably even more important one. In early 2001, while she was in Berlin, Germany, filming *The Cat's Meow*, *Spider-Man* was being cast in Los Angeles—and Dunst was not there to fight for the role.

Bringing a comic book hero to life takes a lot of work, and bringing him to the big screen also takes a lot of time and money. Getting a part in a potential blockbuster, even for a well-known actress like Dunst, is even more challenging. When news broke that a big-screen version of *Spider-Man* was going to be made, there was a buzz in Hollywood. The buzz grew louder when the film's lead was announced: Tobey Maguire, who had recently starred in *The Cider House Rules*, was cast as Peter Parker. Since Maguire was known for playing thoughtful, quiet characters, some people wondered whether he could pull off playing a superhero. Dunst, however, was thrilled with the casting. "I had wanted to work with Tobey for the longest time," Dunst confesses. "I always found something very appealing about him. I just had a feeling we'd be really good onscreen together."[58]

Director Sam Raimi's decision to hire up-and-coming Maguire had actresses scurrying to the casting call for a chance to play his love interest, Mary Jane Watson. "All of the fine young actresses in Hollywood wanted to be Mary Jane Watson once we cast Tobey," Raimi told the *Toronto Star*. "It was great, but we needed somebody who had chemistry with him. We had met Kirsten before we cast him, and I thought she was sweet. Once we got them in the room together, Tobey's pallor seemed to change and he lit up. And as I watched them, I became very involved in their love story."[59]

To get them in a room together, Raimi and Maguire flew all the way to Berlin to the set of *The Cat's Meow*. Dunst had tried out for the role earlier but recalls that fateful final audition:

Director Sam Raimi cast Dunst for the role of Mary Jane Watson in Spider-Man *after she gave a strong audition alongside the film's leading man Tobey Maguire.*

How intimidating, right? And I have three pages to do; two of them are crying scenes. I'd worked since five in the morning and had to get up at five the next day, and here I am in this makeshift meeting room with this little camcorder. I was so nervous. I had to go to the bathroom and have a little breathing session, get focused. I was listening to Coldplay the whole way there, getting myself in a state of mind to be emotional.[60]

Even though Raimi knew he had found his Mary Jane, Dunst was not convinced she had won the sought-after role. It had been three months since she had auditioned with thousands of other actresses, including Kate Hudson, Alicia Witt, Eliza Dushku, Elisha Cuthbert, and Mena Suvari. She had assumed Raimi went with another young actress for the part, but after her impressive audition with Maguire, the role was hers.

Dunst was thrilled for the chance to work with Maguire and Raimi and to play Spider-Man's love interest. Dunst mistakenly thought the hardest part of *Spider-Man*–getting the role–was behind her, but she was now about to learn the difficulties of making an action film.

Getting into Character

Fortunately for Dunst, the one easy thing about making *Spider-Man* was relating to her character, Mary Jane Watson (M.J.). Just like Dunst, M.J. is a young girl from a small town who wants to be an actress. She learns a lot about the world and herself as the film progresses. Dunst told E!Online:

> I was comfortable in Mary Jane's shoes, for sure. And I really wanted to make her a superhero for the girls. She goes on a journey. She didn't have a lot of positive role models in her family, so she falls in with the wrong guys and isn't confident in who she is. I think it takes being at the edge of death to realize what's important in her life and where she wants to be and who she loves.[61]

Because she had not been much of a comic book reader as a kid, preferring Sailor Moon, Lady Lovely Locks, and Rainbow Brite dolls, Dunst read some of the original *Spider-Man*

The "Chemistry" Between Kirsten and Tobey

Even before *Spider-Man* was released, rumors of a romance between the film's two stars were circulating. But Dunst denied that they were more than just good friends. She told the *Toronto Star*:

> The chemistry? Heh, heh, heh. Well, that's why I was hired for the part. We just kind of clicked, and when we did the scenes together, it flowed nicely, I think. There was a magic there that just made everybody in the room kind of disappear a little, like it was just him and I. You're very lucky when you get to be in that kind of situation with an actor and you don't really have to work hard at it. I know there were rumors about us dating, but we're just friends. But if it builds hype about the movie, I just looked at it that way. I know in myself what's true, so whatever, it's OK.

Although rumors of a romance between Tobey Maguire and Dunst circulated during filming of Spider-Man, *Dunst maintained the two were just friends.*

comics to prepare for filming. The natural blonde was also excited to temporarily become a redhead for the part, even if it was only a wig. She told E!Online: "I definitely felt different as a redhead. I felt ballsier and a little bit more serious, a little bit more sexy. It definitely changes your personality when you change your hair color."[62]

The new redhead was eager to start filming. She told E!Online why she thought the film was special:

> *Spider-Man* is probably the most relatable superhero, because he's got the most humanistic qualities of any superhero. He's really a normal guy. What makes him so special is he's charming but a little dorky. You've got the love story in it, and there are great dynamics between the characters. And there are places for us to go and grow in the next movie. It's very based in reality, this story, even though it's got a fantastical thing about it. It really is about these human beings and their relationships.[63]

Making *Spider-Man*

Filming the movie was no small task. Looking back on the months-long making of the action film, Dunst called it her most demanding and difficult project to date because of all the stunts and because many times, as in *Jumanji*, she was acting with no physical props. She explained to zap2it:

> Because there's just so much blue screen [no sets in the background or props]. I was screaming to myself. They put me through more torture than they put Tobey through. I mean, I was doing more stunts than he was. Because you see my face, you can't really hide me. You can hide behind the mask. But I was out in the open, I had to do everything. . . . The best was I had to sit in this chair facing up. The camera was above my head and wiggle my arms and hands and just scream at the camera. It's so ridiculous—you feel like such an idiot. Everybody's around you, like the crew with their doughnuts and their cokes or whatever. And everything's blue around you and here you are falling supposedly.[64]

In the first *Spider-Man* movie, M.J. has almost as many stunts to perform as Spidey, which meant being in peak physical condition. Like the true professionals they are, both Maguire and Dunst dieted and trained daily to be in shape for their parts. Working out and eating right gave Dunst more energy for long days and nights of filming. The strenuous training regimen also made Dunst feel more in control of her body.

However, there were some things about playing M.J. over which Dunst had no control. When director Raimi decided to film a long and pivotal scene between Spider-Man and M.J. in the pouring rain, Dunst had to go along. She said this was actually the hardest scene to film and one of the most awkward, as it was her first kiss with Maguire. She recalled to E!Online:

> It was like, 5 in the morning, birds were starting to chirp. I was nervous to kiss Tobey because it was going to be the first time I kissed him. But then I just went for it. I didn't warn him. I laid it on the boy, and he was impressed,

Dunst claims this scene from Spider-Man, *in which she kisses an upside-down Maguire in the pouring rain, was one of the most difficult to shoot.*

I think. [Laughs hysterically.] But it was not really romantic at all, just kind of awkward. Our situation was awkward, too, because I bunched the mask up under his nose. So during our kiss, he'd be trying to breathe out the side of his mouth. It was not a very good kiss, actually.[65]

Besides all the stunts and the rain, Dunst also found it hard to work with a cast and crew that was primarily comprised of men. Everyone on the set called her "girly-girl," just to get under her skin—and they succeeded: "One day, I was just not in the mood, and the first assistant director was calling me girly girl, and I was like, 'I have a name, it's Kirsten.' But it sucks, because girls are easily called a bitch if they're showing strength. . . . [W]e have to act all sweet."[66] But Dunst rose above the playful teasing, nicely negotiated the stunts, and was excited about the finished product. The cast and crew knew they had a hit on their hands even before filming wrapped.

Along Came a Spider-Man

The film was receiving much publicity and was being touted as *the* box-office hit of the summer before it was released in May 2002, giving Dunst reason to be confident that it would live up to the hype.

As it turned out, Dunst's confidence was justified. The only thing bigger than all the talk surrounding the release of *Spider-Man* on Memorial Day weekend of 2002 was the money the film made. It grossed more than $400 million domestically and more than $750 million internationally. It became the fifth-highest-grossing movie of all time. Even Dunst and her costars were astonished, but they were thrilled with the reception the film received.

Critics praised the film as well. Steve Vineberg of *Christian Century* wrote: "Raimi's refusal to make Spider-Man a comic-book epic is admirable. . . . [W]hen Maguire and Dunst share the screen the movie finds its subject and its heart."[67]

Dunst was especially pleased at the number of females who were seeing the film, which had been dubbed a male-oriented action flick. She said girls thought it was made for guys, but that in truth it was more like a soap opera. Raimi agreed, saying the movie was essentially about a girl. He chose a close-up of Dunst's face—not Maguire's—to adorn the movie's poster.

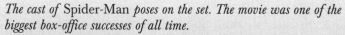

The cast of Spider-Man *poses on the set. The movie was one of the biggest box-office successes of all time.*

Star Treatment

After the release of *Spider-Man*, Dunst became one of the hottest young actresses in Hollywood. At last she could meet her long-time goal of being able to pick and choose her roles, something that few actresses in Hollywood have the opportunity to do. She also began receiving star treatment, including rides on private jets and other perks.

Dunst was now a box-office draw in her own right and a true celebrity. She had to deal with paparazzi following her, chronicling what she ate and where she went, speculating about who she was dating and what designers' clothes she was wearing. It was stressful, but after more than fifteen years in show business, Dunst was prepared for all the attention. She credited her family and friends with keeping her grounded, especially after the release of *Spider-Man*. She told E!Online:

> My mom was always very supportive in my life, and my dad and my grandma and my brother. I think that keeping them all around just sort of keeps you grounded and like a normal human being. It helps you not get caught up in the craziness of this industry. It's important always to keep good, grounded people around you. Good friends and people who aren't so caught up in this business.[68]

With a level head on her shoulders, Dunst was eager to see where her newfound superstar status would take her.

Working with A-List Actresses

Dunst had filmed *Levity*, a film much smaller in scale than *Spider-Man*, starring Billy Bob Thornton, before the release of the blockbuster that made her a household name. In the film, Dunst played a lost party girl, while Thornton's character is a man who has been in prison serving a sentence for murder. Although the movie wasn't a big box-office success and few of Dunsts's fans have even seen the film, she enjoyed working with Thornton, whom she called an amazing person.

It seemed fitting that in her first role after playing Mary Jane, Dunst was cast opposite popular Hollywood leading lady

Julia Roberts in *Mona Lisa Smile*. Interestingly, in addition to Roberts and Dunst, two other hot young female stars, Julia Stiles and Maggie Gyllenhaal, also appeared in this Christmas 2003 release.

In the film, which takes place in the 1950s, Roberts plays a free-thinking art history teacher at Wellesley College, one of the most prestigious all-women's colleges in the United States. All her students, particularly Dunst's Betty, are skeptical of an unmarried female teacher who is dedicated to her career. All of the young women were raised to believe that marriage and children are more important than following any other dreams or

Julia Roberts and Marcia Gay Harden film a scene from the 2003 film Mona Lisa Smile, *in which Dunst also starred.*

ambitions. Roberts's Katherine shows them that it does not have
to be that way.

Betty is the hardest to convince. She goes out of her way to
make Katherine's life at Wellesley difficult. Playing the bratty
girl was a switch for Dunst, who recalls: "Betty was the kind of
role I'd never played before. Betty is so uptight, so narrow-
minded. She doesn't question anything. And as soon as anyone
challenges her, she shuts them right down. She's mean to people, especially [Roberts's character] but it's because she's so un-
happy."[69]

In addition to enjoying her challenging role, Dunst liked getting to know Stiles and Gyllenhaal. Despite rumors of catfights
on the set, the actresses insist that they all got along. "It was way
less dramatic than everybody wants to make it," Gyllenhaal
says. "It was just people who were clear and focused, and good
at what they do, working together on a movie."[70] Adds Stiles:
"We were all very supportive of each other, but that's Acting
101. You want to be good to the people that are in a scene with
you, and vice versa."[71]

Dunst said the trio guzzled Starbucks Coffee, worked on the
New York Times crossword puzzle, and talked about their admiration for costar Roberts. They also discussed their characters,
and Stiles and Gyllenhaal talked about their own experiences
with college professors. Stiles and Gyllenhaal, both Columbia
University grads, made Dunst reconsider going to college one
day. "Being around Julia and Maggie and talking about college
professors does make me think about wanting to take classes,"
says Dunst. "It's important to always be interested in finding out
the origins of why we do what we do."[72]

While making Mona Lisa Smile was exciting for Dunst, reviews for the film were not very enthusiastic. Amy Feitelberg of
Entertainment Weekly wrote: "Ladies, if you want to believe that
there's more to college than getting your MRS., grab your lip-
stick and heed this warning: Do not see Mona Lisa Smile. It will
insult your intelligence."[73] Rolling Stone said: "Not a . . . thing to
smile about."[74]

Fortunately for Dunst, her career was not affected by Smile,
which was considered a flop. She seemed above even the fail-

Cast and crew members of Mona Lisa Smile *pose at a Hollywood screening in December 2003. Although Dunst enjoyed making the film, it was a flop at the box-office.*

ures. Although she was incredibly successful even by Hollywood standards, Dunst was modest about her stardom. She respects the work of colleagues, even on her films that were not well received, and takes pride in her work, successful or not.

Ensemble Acting

The newly minted leading lady surprised Hollywood by taking a smaller supporting role in the critically acclaimed *Eternal Sunshine of the Spotless Mind.* In the film, Jim Carrey and Kate Winslet play two ex-lovers who decide to undergo a new surgical procedure to erase each other from their minds. They want it to be as if their love never happened, but along the way they learn that the past should not be forgotten. The offbeat drama/comedy/romance/sci-fi film was a departure for Dunst, and her turn as Mary offered her yet another change of pace.

Dunst was proving her versatility in Hollywood, which was just her intention. She explains: "A lot of people still try to put you in a box. They see one movie of yours and they don't think you can play this type of role or that type of role."[75] After making so many different kinds of movies and playing so many different characters, Dunst had more than proved she could play any kind of character she wanted.

Chapter 6

An Eye on the Future

As a young woman in her twenties, Dunst was ready to focus on longevity in her career. Other young adults start to think about postgraduation plans at her age, and Dunst was ready to make some changes as well. She took control of the off-screen side of her career, hiring a new agent (leaving children's agent Burton after a decade) and a publicist—a new necessity considering all the press she was receiving—Steven Huvane, who also represents Jennifer Aniston. Dunst saw herself as an adult after making *Spider-Man* and wanted to have people working for her and with her who were not tempted to continue treating her like a little girl. She started proactively reading more scripts and taking more of an interest in her finances, which she had previously left up to her financial adviser.

And after nearly twenty years in show business, she was also more outspoken about the characters she played. She asked that her part in *Spider-Man 2* be less damsel-in-distress and more independent woman. Her storyline was central to the new film. Dunst also kept up the trend of mixing up her roles, adding period pieces to contemporary love stories and blockbuster action movies. She hoped that by choosing roles intelligently, she would have at least another twenty years of acting before her.

Wooden Spoon Productions

Part of Dunst's plan to make a lasting impact in Hollywood had originated while she was still a teen but did not gain steam until she had acquired more clout in the business. Dunst and her mother started a film company, Wooden Spoon Productions, to choose and produce quality films especially for women. Dunst knew she had been fortunate in her career and with the roles she played. "I've been lucky because it's hard for kids to make a transition into adult roles," she says. "But I did films that would challenge me and help me grow. It was all about what was going to be best for me in the long run."[76]

The company's name honors Dunst's grandmother, who used to take out a wooden spoon and shake it at the kids when they misbehaved, though Dunst is quick to point out that she never actually hit them with it. The name reflects the strength of women, a subject Dunst feels passionately about. She thinks fe-

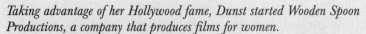

Taking advantage of her Hollywood fame, Dunst started Wooden Spoon Productions, a company that produces films for women.

What the Critics Say . . .

Some film critics have praised Dunst's acting ability. Reporter Tom Carson is one. In "Onward Kirsten Soldiers" in the November 2001 issue of *Esquire* magazine Carson expresses admiration for her talents:

> [Dunst] grasps each role so completely on its own terms that her behavior is utterly idiomatic; only later does it sink in how intuitively to the point her performance has been. . . . Dunst has a knack for making her characters' thought processes so understandable that it's impossible to stay out of sympathy with their motives. Even in her frothiest movies, she doesn't play airheads; she plays young women who don't know they've got brains.

male stars should get billing over their male costars if theirs is the leading role. But in order for this to happen, there needs to be more good leading roles for young actresses to play. So Dunst and Inez read lots of scripts, carefully selecting those they would like to work on. Inez offers her valuable opinion but is careful to let her daughter make her own decisions. Dunst is grateful to have her mother by her side helping her with her business. "Even when I think I am at the age past needing my mother, I still want her there,"[77] Dunst admits.

Coming of age and having her own business made Dunst feel gutsier and more accomplished than ever before. No longer a teenager, she identified more with admired, experienced actresses such as Gwyneth Paltrow and Kate Winslet, who had grown up in show business. She also looked to these women for advice and guidance with her career. Dunst explained to *Cosmo-Girl*: "I feel like I can call them up and say, 'Listen, I'm going through such and such—what did you do? When I went back to do the second Spider-Man, I built a better relationship with the director, I got to know everybody better, and I just felt better being on the set. And I think that's all just a part of becoming a woman."[78]

Preparing for *Spider-Man 2*

Building a better relationship with Raimi served Dunst well. Mary Jane's storyline was central to the plot of *Spider-Man 2*.

She talked to the director and expressed her concerns for the sequel: "'Can I scream less this time?' [she asked]. In the end Spider-Man has to save me, but Mary Jane's much more grown up, much more developed in this one."[79] And she had even more fun filming the sequel because she was comfortable with the other actors, especially Maguire, who has nothing but praise for his costar and rumored ex-girlfriend. He says:

> She's not very self-conscious in front of the camera or off-screen. She exposes her true self, which is very admirable. What is that quote? I think it's from [the film] Dangerous Liaisons: "Vanity and happiness cannot coexist." She's a happy girl. She's not worried about that stuff. If you're too involved in "How do I Iook?" then you're too preoccupied to live and be free. She . . . [is] a really sweet, aware, open person, who's really talented, knows how to focus her energy and makes intelligent decisions beyond her years.[80]

Dunst was equally enthusiastic about working with Maguire again. He was a big reason behind her desire to play the role. "I thought he was a really interesting choice for Spider-Man," she says. "Normally when they're trying to make comic books into movies, they just want these bulked-up guys who look good in action scenes. But Tobey is an actor. That told me they were looking at doing something different."[81]

That something different was a movie trilogy (the *Spider-Man* series) that appeals to both men and women. Dunst was not interested in making a movie that was only for men. *Spider-Man*, says Dunst, "is a movie for chicks. You can throw in all the action and fighting you want, but it's still a love story. . . . It's still about the guy wanting to get the girl. . . . I wouldn't be in it if there weren't something for the girls. I don't like films that exclude people."[82]

In the sequel, Peter Parker gets a little closer to getting the girl, but not without a struggle. He is now a college student who can not keep up with his classes or his job and has little social life because of the time he puts in as Spider-Man. So he gives up his Spidey suit and tries to live a normal life. But he is compelled to

Tobey Maguire and Kirsten film a scene from Spider-Man 2. *Both actors were excited at the prospect of working together in the sequel.*

get back in costume when a tentacled creature dubbed Doc Ock starts rampaging through the city. Mary Jane is still in love with Peter, but is ready to give up on him and marry an astronaut who has proposed to her. "Mary Jane's always with the cool guy who's wrong for her but is handsome, maybe with more money,"[83] Dunst notes. But her heart is with Peter—and she is, too, by the movie's end.

The Filming Starts

By April of 2003 the script was written and both Maguire and Dunst were excited by the storyline and ready to start filming. But then, Maguire almost backed out of the picture after incurring back injuries while playing jockey Red Pollard in the movie *Seabiscuit.* He was worried about all the stunts he would have to perform and wanted the shooting schedule (which had already been set) to be reworked. Studio executives incorrectly assumed that Maguire was trying to exact a higher price for his services and were about to offer the role to actor Jake Gyllenhaal, who was then Dunst's boyfriend. Although Dunst would have been thrilled to work with Jake, she knew Maguire was the one and only Spider-Man. "When Tobey wasn't going to do it, well, that was a hard time," says Dunst. "I think it really needed to be Tobey, because that's Peter Parker, and he is Spider-Man, so it was scary."[84]

Fortunately, Maguire reconsidered and made the film. He was happy with his decision and insisted that his reluctance had nothing to do with the salary offered. Filming went even smoother than the first and he never suffered any injuries. Maguire says, "[But] it ended up being not so bad. The harnesses were better, the wires were smoother, and the stunts, I think, were easier."[85]

Spider-Man saves Mary Jane in a scene from Spider-Man 2. *Although Spider-Man must still save M.J., Dunst insisted her character be more self-reliant in the sequel.*

What was not easy was the shooting schedule, a long and grueling six months during a hot summer with heavy costumes and lots of sweaty stunts. When Dunst got a call just two months before the film's release that she was needed for a reshoot of a scene, she had no choice but to get back into character, even though she was ready to be finished with the film. The never-ending schedule had Dunst joking about the future of her character in the last film. "I always say I want to die in *Spider-Man 3*," she laughs. "I think it would be so fun to die a really cinematic death—like Spider-Man accidentally runs [M.J.] into a wall."[86]

However, that does not seem a likely ending for the third and final installment. Fans want to see Peter and Mary Jane end up together. *Spider-Man 2* grossed more than $370 million and was the second-highest-grossing film of 2004, breaking the record for the highest opening-day gross (more than $40 million). There would seem to be a large ready-made audience for *Spider- Man 3*, slated for release in May 2007.

Dunst's Love Life

After the successful release of *Spider-Man 2* and the subsequent huge profits and positive reviews, Dunst was riding high. She was also head over heels in love with Jake Gyllenhaal, the younger brother of her *Mona Lisa Smile* costar Maggie Gyllenhaal. The two had started dating in September 2002 after Maggie introduced them, and the happy pair were photographed everywhere together, holding hands and kissing, drinking coffee and whispering to each other, and walking their dog, Atticus.

Dunst told *People* magazine: "I'm really happy and in love."[87] The couple even bought a $1.7-million house in Los Angeles, adopted a cat, gave each other promise rings, and moved in together. There were rumors that a wedding was not far behind. However, the crazy schedules of the two actors and much interaction in the public eye took their toll on the relationship. The arrangement would have been difficult for any couple to maintain.

Late in the summer of 2004, news surfaced that the couple had called it quits. Dunst first denied the split, then claimed they were taking time off. "We're both young," she told *Teen Vogue*. "I'm 22—I'm going to be with different guys. But he's my best

Dunst has had an on-again, off-again relationship with actor Jake Gyllenhaal for over two years.

friend and none of those feelings have changed."[88] And indeed the two were spotted lunching together weeks later. In the fall of 2004, photos of Dunst and Gyllenhaal shopping together and kissing were printed in magazines, and there were stories of a reconciliation. They were back together and appeared to be a happy couple again.

As for the initial breakup, there were rumors that the couple had different views as to how to spend what little free time they both had. A friend of Dunst's told *US Weekly*: "She hasn't gotten partying out of her system yet, and [Jake] has. She wants to have fun. When Jake goes out with Kirsten and her friends to dinner or something, Kirsten will want to go out afterward to a club. Jake will go home."[89] Dunst was by then linked to another costar, Orlando Bloom, with whom she was making *Elizabeth-town*. They were seen together at bars all over Lexington, Kentucky, where the movie was filmed. While their relationship was never confirmed, Dunst did decide to keep her off-screen life private. And indeed, her relationship with Gyllenhaal seems to be less chronicled in the media.

Tennis Pro

Despite her determination to decrease the visibility of her private life, she was anxious that her career still be discussed in the

For her role in the 2004 romantic comedy Wimbledon, *Kirsten had to learn how to play tennis like a pro.*

media and that audiences would come to her films. Dunst had been to cheerleader boot camp for *Bring It On*, and now she was ready for another kind of intensive training. This time she needed to learn how to be a great tennis player for the romantic comedy *Wimbledon*. The movie also provided her biggest paycheck to date: She reportedly received $5 million for the film. Money aside, Dunst wanted to be convincing as a tennis player, so she spent three months throwing herself into learning to serve

Kirsten smiles next to a promotional poster at the Hollywood premiere of Wimbledon. *She reportedly earned $5 million for her work in the film.*

and volley like a pro, and developing what one observer calls an "awesome backhand."[90]

In the film, Dunst plays Lizzie Bradbury, an aggressive up-and-coming player with a divalike temper and a domineering father. She is surprised to find herself falling for an aging British tennis player, played by Paul Bettany.

The film, which was released in September 2004, garnered some good reviews. Thelma Adams of *US Weekly* wrote:

> The dimpled Dunst aces the question of which young actress might be the next Julia Roberts. Now a movie veteran, the Spider-Man beauty effortlessly serves up mainstream romantic comedy that's unafraid to have a goofy, soft center. And the camera loves her too! She and Bettany have an electric chemistry that lacks any strain (or gratuitous nudity). Together, they deliver a satisfying and optimistic love-me duo in which the audience can't help but root for the charming lovers to come—and stay—together.[91]

Despite good reviews and fun with filming, Dunst admitted that she did not want to pick up a tennis racket for a long time to come. She was, however, happy with the film, which she called "really cute—the perfect date-night movie."[92]

Elizabethtown and Beyond

Her next project took her to the Southern town of Lexington, Kentucky, to film Cameron Crowe's *Elizabethtown*. In the movie, Dunst plays a flight attendant who strikes up an unexpected romance with Orlando Bloom's character during a memorial service. Dunst describes the film as crossing over the genres of comedy and drama, making it more like life, which is full of both funny and poignant moments. Dunst praised Crowe for pulling it off, saying, "Cameron really gets those intimate moments between people."[93] Dunst was thrilled to work with writer and director Crowe, whose *Almost Famous*, a big hit in 2000, was a project she had hoped to be cast in.

For her next role, Dunst knew she had another challenge on her hands. She was going to play the sole lead in Sofia Coppola's *Marie Antoinette*. In the film, slated for release in early 2006, Dunst will be called on to give a convincing impression of the eighteenth-century European monarch. To this end, she planned to spend the winter of 2004 studying French to play the woman who became the controversial queen in 1774 and was guillotined in 1793.

Coppola was thrilled to work with Dunst again, as was Kirsten with Sofia. The two had admired each other while filming *The Virgin Suicides*. In addition to writing the script based on British historian Antonia Fraser's biography of the queen, Coppola was set to direct and coproduce the project. She also cast her cousin, actor Jason Schwartzman, as King Louis XVI. The movie will no doubt prove to be a learning experience for Dunst, who loves to read and makes it a point to learn about history for period pieces she makes. But she mostly welcomed how different this new movie was from *Elizabethtown* and *Spider-Man 2*.

To Dunst, variety is the spice of her career and the reason she keeps acting after all these years. "I've been acting since I was 3," she says. "That's a long time to do any job. If I don't try different things, I'd go crazy. . . . After doing a movie with so much action and special effects [like *Spider-Man*], you kind of want to do a

Kirsten's Political Views

Dunst has very definite views on politics and urges everyone to vote. In commenting on the Bush administration's record on the environment, she told the *Times* of London: "We're not planning for the future for our kids. We're totally screwing ourselves, which is depressing." Kirsten hopes she makes movies that not only entertain young people but educate them to take action. "I can make an impact, because I am an actress, and if I can make a movie that will make people think about things, then great."

In October 2004 Kirsten joined the Women on the Move bus tour, a group of celebrities that included Ashley Judd and Julia Louis-Dreyfus, campaigning on behalf of Democratic Party presidential candidate John Kerry. They visited towns all across America to encourage people to consider the issues affecting them, such as health care and reproductive rights, and to vote for Kerry. As a new voter, Kirsten was specifically hoping to influence young people to get out and vote. In the weeks before the November 2004 election, she made numerous public appearances in Michigan, Florida, and California to rally young voters and stump for Kerry.

Dunst actively encouraged young people to vote in the 2004 presidential election. Here, she shows her support for presidential hopeful John Kerry at a Florida rally.

small, quiet one. I just want to keep pushing myself. I've been doing this most of my life, but I've still got a lot to learn."[94]

In her personal life, Dunst would love to get married and have children. She told *People* magazine when she was only twelve: "I want to be an actress for practically all of my life. I want two children and a house overlooking Sunset Boulevard."[95] Whether these wishes come true, only time will tell. But Kirsten Dunst has wishes for her nearer future as well. She told *Rolling Stone*:

> I wish I had more downtime. I love to paint, to write, to learn acoustic guitar and French and Italian. I want to go backpacking with my friends in Europe. I want to go on *Crossing Over With John Edward*. I'd like to be regressed to find out about my past lives, because I feel I've been around a couple of times on this earth. I'd like to sing a

Kirsten Dunst has a very bright future ahead of her. As one of Hollywood's top actresses, Dunst can expect to play a variety of roles for years to come.

torch song like Peggy Lee sings "Fever." And I'd like to play a serial killer.[96]

As for what is next on the career front, there was a buzz around Hollywood that Dunst may play a teenage prostitute in *Crimson Petal.* And then there is *Spider-Man 3,* slated for a May 2007 release. She has also expressed an interest in getting behind the camera and directing someday. Whatever road she chooses, Kirsten's fans are sure to enjoy her talents for years to come.

Notes

Chapter 1: Already Acting

1. Quoted in Dan Santow and Leah Feldon-Mitchell, "Knocking 'Em Dead," *People*, November 28, 1994, p. 110.
2. Quoted in Michael Sauter, "The Natural: Kirsten Dunst," *Biography*, August 2002, p. 92.
3. Quoted in Sauter, "The Natural: Kirsten Dunst," p. 92.
4. Quoted in Sauter, "The Natural: Kirsten Dunst," p. 93.
5. Quoted in Sauter, "The Natural: Kirsten Dunst," p. 93.
6. Quoted in David Eimer, "Bliss of the Spider-Woman," *The Times* (London), July 10, 1994, features section, p. 15.
7. Quoted in David A. Keeps, "Kirsten Dunst Busts Out," *Rolling Stone*, May 23, 2002, p. 67.
8. Quoted in Barry Koltnow, "'Jeopardy' Helped Kirsten Dunst Land Role in 'Drop Dead Gorgeous.'" *Orange County Register*, July 21, 1999.
9. Quoted in Santow and Feldon-Mitchell, "Knocking 'Em Dead," p. 111.
10. Quoted in Santow and Feldon-Mitchell, "Knocking 'Em Dead," p. 111.
11. Quoted in Sauter, "The Natural: Kirsten Dunst," p. 93.
12. Quoted in Santow and Feldon-Mitchell, "Knocking 'Em Dead," p. 111.
13. Quoted in David A. Keeps, "The Temptations of Kirsten Dunst," *Rolling Stone*, July 19, 2001, p. 44.
14. Quoted in David Keeps, "The 25 Hottest Stars Under 25," *Teen People*, June/July 2002, p. 99.

15. Tom Gliatto and David Hiltbrand, "Interview with the Vampire," *People*, November 21, 1994, p. 21.

Chapter 2: Teen Star

16. Leah Rozen, "Jumanji," *People*, December 18, 1995, p. 21.
17. Quoted in Rebecca Ascher-Walsh, "Jumanji," *Entertainment Weekly*, August 25, 1995–September 1, 1995, p. 62.
18. Quoted in Ascher-Walsh, "Jumanji," p. 62.
19. Quoted in Keeps, "The Temptations of Kirsten Dunst," p. 44.
20. Quoted in Deanna Kizis, "Kirsten Dunst Wants to Show You . . . ," *Cosmopolitan*, April 2001, p. 196.
21. Quoted in Keeps, "The Temptations of Kirsten Dunst," p. 44.
22. Quoted in Kirk Hawkins, "The Leading Lady," *Teen People*, March 2001, p. 126.
23. Quoted in Sauter, "The Natural: Kirsten Dunst," p. 94.

Chapter 3: Independent Spirit

24. Quoted in Koltnow, "'Jeopardy' Helped Kirsten Dunst Land Role."
25. Quoted in Koltnow, "'Jeopardy' Helped Kirsten Dunst Land Role."
26. Quoted in Julie Jordan, "Spotlight on . . . Kirsten Dunst," *People*, August 23, 1999, p. 41.
27. Quoted in Lauren Waterman, "Her Time Is Now," *Teen Vogue*, October 2004, p. 157.
28. Quoted in Amanda Rudolph, "Jammin' With the A-Teen," *InStyle*, April 1999, p. 322.
29. *Rolling Stone*, "Chick Flicks with a Vengeance," April 27, 2000, p. 80.
30. Karen Hershenson, "The Virgin Suicides," *Contra Costa Times*, April 20, 2000.
31. Glen Lovell, "The Virgin Suicides," *San Jose Mercury News*, April 20, 2000.
32. The Virgin Suicides Interview: Kirsten Dunst. http://www.paramountclassics.com/virginsuicides/html_3/index.html.
33. The Virgin Suicides Interview: Kirsten Dunst.
34. Quoted in Kizis, "Kirsten Dunst Wants to Show You . . . ," p. 196.
35. Quoted in Kizis, "Kirsten Dunst Wants to Show You . . . ," p. 196.

Chapter 4: Breaking the Mold

36. Quoted in Devin Rose, "'Bring It On' Puts the 'Ugh' in Ugly," *Chicago Tribune*, August 31, 2000.

37. Steven Rea, "Bring It On," *Philadelphia Inquirer*, August 23, 2000.

38. Rose, "Bring It On Puts the 'Ugh' in Ugly."

39. Quoted in Waterman, "Her Time Is Now," p. 161.

40. Quoted in Claudia Puig, "Stars of 'Mona Lisa' Smile on Their Good Fortune," *USA Today*, December 18, 2003.

41. Quoted in Waterman, "Her Time Is Now," p. 161.

42. Quoted in Kizis, "Kirsten Dunst Wants to Show You . . . ," p. 199.

43. *Teen People*, "It Girl," Febraury 2001, p. 46.

44. Quoted in Kizis, "Kirsten Dunst Wants to Show You . . . ," p. 199.

45. Quoted in Keeps, "The Temptations of Kirsten Dunst," p. 44.

46. Quoted in Jess Cagle, "Beyond Teen Tricks," *Time Canada*, July 2, 2001, p. 56.

47. Quoted in Cagle, "Beyond Teen Tricks," p. 56.

48. Quoted in Andrew Rodgers, "Nudity Is Tasteless Says 'Crazy' Star Kirsten Dunst," zap2it.com, June 27, 2001. http://www.zap2it.com/movies/news/story/0,1259,---7265,00.html.

49. Quoted in Kizis, "Kirsten Dunst Wants to Show You . . . ," p. 199.

50. Quoted in Keeps, "The Temptations of Kirsten Dunst," p. 44.

51. Quoted in Kizis, "Kirsten Dunst Wants to Show You. . . ."

52. Quoted in Cagle, "Beyond Teen Tricks," p. 56.

53. Steven Rea, "Crazy/Beautiful," *Philadelphia Inquirer*, June 28, 2001.

54. David Willoughby, "Crazy/Beautiful," *The Times*, June 1, 2001.

Chapter 5: The Big Time

55. Quoted in Kizis, "Kirsten Dunst Wants to Show You . . . ," p. 199.

56. Quoted in H.W. Fowler, "Spidey's Girl Gets Animated on Kissing Tobey, Being a Girly-Girl and Turning the Big 2-0," E!Online. http://www.eonline.com/Features/Features/Spiderman/Dunst QA/.

57. Tom Carson, "Onward Kirsten Soldiers," *Esquire*, November 2001, p. 72.

58. Quoted in Keeps, "Kirsten Dunst Busts Out," p. 64.

59. Quoted in Bob Strauss, "Dunst Charms Both Spiders and Cats," *Toronto Star*, May 8, 2002.

60. Quoted in Fowler, "Spidey's Girl Gets Animated."

61. Quoted in Fowler, "Spidey's Girl Gets Animated."

62. Quoted in Fowler, "Spidey's Girl Gets Animated."

63. Quoted in Fowler, "Spidey's Girl Gets Animated."

64. Quoted in Andrew Rodgers, "Kirsten Dunst Dangles 'Spider-Man' Secrets," zap2it.com, July 13, 2001. http://www.zap2it.com/movies/news/story/0,1259,-7582,00.html.

65. Quoted in Fowler, "Spidey's Girl Gets Animated."

66. Quoted in Fowler, "Spidey's Girl Gets Animated."

67. Steve Vineberg, "To Kiss a Spider," *Christian Century*, May 22, 2002, p. 48.

68. Quoted in Fowler, "Spidey's Girl Gets Animated."

69. Community CustomWire, "Dunst Relishes Bad Girl Role," December 24, 2003, p. 83.

70. Quoted in Puig, "Stars of 'Mona Lisa' Smile on Their Good Fortune."

71. Quoted in Puig, "Stars of 'Mona Lisa' Smile on Their Good Fortune."

72. Quoted in Puig, "Stars of 'Mona Lisa' Smile on Their Good Fortune."

73. Amy Feitelberg, "Mona Lisa Smile," *Entertainment Weekly*, March 12, 2004, p. 99.

74. Peter Travers, "Mona Lisa Smile," *Rolling Stone*, January 22, 2004, p. 77.

75. Quoted in Puig, "Stars of 'Mona Lisa' Smile on Their Good Fortune."

Chapter 6: An Eye on the Future

76. Quoted in Keeps, "25 Hottest Stars Under 25," p. 99.

77. Quoted in Jordan, "Spotlight On . . . Kirsten Dunst," p. 41.

78. Quoted in Joanne Gordon and Lauren Brown, "'03 CosmoGirl! of the Year," *CosmoGirl!*, December 2003–January 2004, p. 114.

79. Quoted in Eimer, "Bliss of the Spider-Woman."

80. Quoted in Keeps, "Kirsten Dunst Busts Out," p. 62.

81. Quoted in Scott Bowles, "Step into My Parlor, Says This Fly Girl," *USA Today*, May 6, 2002.

82. Quoted in Bowles, "Step into My Parlor, Says This Fly Girl."

83. Quoted in Bowles, "Step into My Parlor, Says This Fly Girl."

84. Quoted in Rebecca Ascher-Walsh, "Arach Is Back," *Entertainment Weekly*, April 30, 2004, p. 34.

85. Quoted in Ascher-Walsh, "Arach Is Back," p. 34.

86. Quoted in Ascher-Walsh, "Arach Is Back," p. 34.

87. Quoted in Greg Adkins et al., "Split: Kirsten and Jake," *People*, August 2, 2004, p. 21.

88. Quoted in Waterman, "Her Time Is Now," p. 161.

89. Quoted in *US Weekly*, "Kirsten: Back on the Market!" August 9, 2004, p. 44.

90. Quoted in Waterman, "Her Time Is Now," p. 161.

91. Thelma Adams, "Wimbledon," *US Weekly*, September 27, 2004, p. 88.

92. Quoted in Waterman, "Her Time Is Now," p. 161.

93. Quoted in Waterman, "Her Time Is Now," p. 161.

94. Quoted in Bowles, "Step into My Parlor, Says This Fly Girl."

95. Quoted in Santow and Feldon-Mitchell, "Knocking 'Em Dead," p. 110.

96. Quoted in Keeps, "The Temptations of Kirsten Dunst," p. 44.

Important Dates in the Life of Kirsten Dunst

April 30, 1982
Kirsten Caroline Dunst is born in Point Pleasant, New Jersey, a small seaside town one hundred miles south of New York City.

1985
Dunst signs with Elite Modeling Agency and begins appearing in print ads and television commercials.

1989
Dunst has a bit role in her first movie, *New York Stories*; more small roles follow.

1990
Kirsten, her mother, and her brother move to Los Angeles.

1994
Interview with a Vampire is released and Dunst becomes nationally known. She is nominated for a Golden Globe award for her performance. *Little Women* with Winona Ryder and Susan Sarandon is released.

1995
Dunst wins YoungStar Award, MTV Movie Award, and Saturn Award for her performance in *Interview*. Appears in *Jumanji* with Robin Williams.

1998
Dunst appears in *Wag the Dog* and stars in the acclaimed made-for-television drama *Fifteen and Pregnant*.

1999

Dunst appears in the films *Dick* and *Drop Dead Gorgeous.*

2000

Dunst graduates from Notre Dame High School in Los Angeles. Following a string of unsatisfying and forgettable films, she vows to make fewer, higher-quality projects. *The Virgin Suicides* is released.

2001

Dunst stars in *Get Over It* and *crazy/beautiful,* a role that forces her out of her bubbly, girl-next-door image.

2002

Spider-Man is released and Dunst becomes a blockbuster draw and international star.

2003

Important roles include *Mona Lisa Smile* with Julia Roberts and *Levity* with Billy Bob Thornton.

2004

Dunst has supporting role in *Eternal Sunshine of the Spotless Mind*; reprises role of Mary Jane in *Spider-Man 2*; stars in *Wimbledon.*

2005

Dunst stars in Cameron Crowe's *Elizabethtown* opposite actor Orlando Bloom.

For Further Reading

Books

Mark Vas, *Behind the Mask of Spider-Man: The Secrets of the Movie*. New York: Del Rey, 2002.

——, *Caught in the Web: Dreaming Up the World of Spider-Man 2*. New York: Del Rey, 2004.

Periodicals

Lauren Waterman, "Her Time Is Now," *Teen Vogue*, October 2004.

Web Sites

Kirsten Dunst, Internet Movie Database (http://www.imdb.com/name/nm0000379/). Devoted to Kirsten's films, this site includes a bio and extensive list of credits.

kirsten-dunst.org (http://www.kirsten-dunst.org). This fan page devoted to Kirsten features a biography, filmography, articles about the actress, and more fan info.

KirstenFan.com (http://www.kirstenfan.com). Another detailed Kirsten fan site that contains a biography, a filmography, and more fan information.

Works Consulted

Periodicals

Thelma Adams, "Wimbledon," *US Weekly*, September 27, 2004.

Greg Adkins et al. "Split: Kirsten and Jake," *People*, August 2, 2004.

Rebecca Asher-Walsh, "Arach Is Back," *Entertainment Weekly*, April 30, 2004.

——, "Jumanji," *Entertainment Weekly*, August 25, 1995–September 1, 1995.

Scott Bowles, "Step into My Parlor, Says This Fly Girl," *USA Today*, May 6, 2002.

Al Brumley, "Crazy/Beautiful Takes Chances on Its Out-of-Control Heroine," *Dallas Morning News*, November 20, 2001.

Jess Cagle, "Beyond Teen Tricks," *Time Canada*, July 2, 2001.

Tom Carson, "Onward Kirsten Soldiers," *Esquire*, November 2001.

Paul Coco, "Power Pair," *Scholastic Scope*, May 6, 2002.

Community CustomWire, "Dunst Relishes Bad Girl Role," December 24, 2003.

David Eimer, "Bliss of the Spider-Woman," *The Times* (London), July 10, 2004.

Amy Feitelberg, "Mona Lisa Smile," *Entertainment Weekly*, March 12, 2004.

Tom Gliatto, "Interview With a Vampire," *People*, November 21, 1994.

Joanne Gordon and Lauren Brown, "'03 Cosmo Girl of the Year," *CosmoGirl!*, December 2003–January 2004.

Sara Graham, "Kirsten Dunst," *Teen People*, June/July 2004.

Kirk Hawkins, "The Leading Lady," *Teen People*, March 2001.

Karen Hershenson, "The Virgin Suicides," *Contra Costa Times*, April 20, 2000.

Ross Johnson, "Kirsten Dunst," *Esquire*, June 2002.

Julie Jordan, "Spotlight on . . . Kirsten Dunst," *People*, August 23, 1999.

David A. Keeps, "The Temptations of Kirsten Dunst," *Rolling Stone*, July 19, 2001.

——, "Kirsten Dunst Busts Out," *Rolling Stone*, May 23, 2002.

——, "25 Hottest Stars Under 25," *Teen People*, June/July 2002.

Deanna Kizis, "Kirsten Dunst Wants to Show You . . . ," *Cosmopolitan*, April 2001.

Barry Koltnow, "'Jeopardy' Helped Kirsten Dunst Land Role in 'Drop Dead Gorgeous,'" *Orange County Register*, July 21, 1999.

Glen Lovell, "The Virgin Suicides," *San Jose Mercury News*, April 20, 2000.

Sarah Mower, "Kirsten Dunst," *Harper's Bazaar*, September 1999.

Claudia Puig, "Stars of 'Mona Lisa' Smile on Their Good Fortune," *USA Today*, December 18, 2003.

Steven Rea, "Bring It On," *Philadelphia Inquirer*, August 23, 2000.

——, "Crazy/Beautiful," *Philadelphia Inquirer*, June 28, 2001.

Rolling Stone, "Chick Flicks With a Vengeance," April 27, 2000.

Devin Rose, "'Bring It On' Puts the 'Ugh' in Ugly," *Chicago Tribune*, August 31, 2000.

Leah Rozen, "Jumanji," *People*, December 18, 1995.

—— "Little Women," *People*, January 1, 1995.

Amanda Rudolph, "Jammin' With the A-Teen," *InStyle*, April 1999.

Dan Santow, "Knocking 'Em Dead," *People*, November 28, 1994.

Michael Sauter, "The Natural: Kirsten Dunst," *Biography*, August 2000.

Lisa Schwarzbaum, "Sister Act," *Entertainment Weekly*, December 23, 1994.

Jennifer L. Smith, "Along Came a Spider-Man," *Teen People*, October 2001.

Bob Strauss, "Dunst Charms Both Spiders and Cats," *Toronto Star*, May 8, 2002.

Teen People, "It Girl," February 2001.

Peter Travers, "Mona Lisa Smile," *Rolling Stone*, January 22, 2004.

US Weekly, "Kirsten: Back on the Market!" August 9, 2004.

Steve Vineberg, "To Kiss a Spider," *Christian Century*, May 22, 2002.

David Willoughby, "Crazy/Beautiful," *The Times*, June 1, 2001.

Internet Sources

Asena Basak, "Kirsten Dunst on Kissing Older Guys," Zap2It.com, April 22, 2002. www.zap2it.com/movies/news/story/0,1259, ---11962,00.htm.

H.W. Fowler, "Spidey's Girl Gets Animated on Kissing Tobey, Being a Girly-Girl and Turning the Big 2-0." E!Online. http:// www.eonline.com/Features/Features/Spiderman/DunstQA/.

Andrew Rodgers, "Kirsten Dunst Dangles Spider-Man Secrets,"
Zap2It.com, July 6, 2001. http://www.zap2it.com/movies/
news/story/0,1259,-7582,00.html.

——, "Nudity Is Tasteless, Says 'Crazy' Star Kirsten Dunst," Zap2It.
com, June 26, 2001. http://www.zap2it.com/movies/news/
story/0,1259,---7265,00.html.

The Virgin Suicides Interview: Kirsten Dunst. http://www.
paramountclassics.com/virginsuicides/html_3/index.html.

Index

Picture Credits

About the Author

Award-winning author Anne E. Hill has written numerous biographies and fiction books for young readers, including four titles in Lucent's People in the News series: *Sandra Bullock, Drew Barrymore, Sting,* and *Reese Witherspoon.* Some of her other biographies include *Cameron Diaz, Gwyneth Paltrow, Michelle Kwan,* and *Denzel Washington.* She has also written two fiction books for a popular teen series.

Hill graduated magna cum laude with a bachelor's degree in English from Franklin and Marshall College in 1996, where she was a member of the Phi Beta Kappa Society. She lives outside of Philadelphia with her husband George and son Caleb.